6 JUNE 1944
SOLDIERS IN NORMANDY

Compiled by Philippe CHARBONNIER

Translated by Yves J. Van Keer (American Paratroopers),
A. Godenne (British Paratroopers) and
Jean-Pierre Villaume (the 'Hitlerjugend' Division and the GI of D-Day).

Jacques	ALLUCHON		Jean	de LAGARDE
Pierre	BESNARD		Jon	GAWNE
Jean	BOUCHERY		Patrick	NONZERVILLE
Philippe	CHARBONNIER		Eric	LEFEVRE
Marcus	COTTON		Bernard	PETITJEAN
Christophe	DESCHODT		Yves	TARIEL

ISBN: 2 908 182 327
HISTOIRE ET COLLECTIONS, P.O. Box 327, Poole, Dorset BH 15 2RG UK

CONTENTS

This remarkable photograph was taken on 6 June, a short distance away from the beachhead. It depicts a first-aid post set up by the medical unit of the Engineer Special Brigade to care for and process wounded soldiers. The insignia of the ESBse appears on the sleeve of the medic at right who is busy filling out the evacuation forms which specify the wounds and condition of each soldier. This data will be of great assistance to the staff of hospitals in Britain who will attend the casualties after their transport across the channel.

Quite predictably, many paratroopers from the 82nd and 101st Airborne Divisions, are among the casualties. Few appear to be wounded and it looks as though most of them are suffering from exhaustion after spending the night looking for their unit or objectives. To boost morale, the significance of the role played by US airborne troops on 6 June was overrated, but recent research shows that the paras were hardly more successful during 'Overlord' than they were in the Sicily and Italy campaigns.

Not all the M-1942 jump uniforms shown here have been reinforced with canvas, and some paras are wearing garrison caps adorned with the Airborne troops' badge. (*National Archives via JYN*).

In the evening of June 5, 1944: grinning to hide his anxiety, 'Ike' talks with some men of the 502nd P.I.R. on their base at Newbury, Berkshire. *'What about tou, you Private, what will you do when the war is over ?'. At the moment, Sir, my prime concern is to return to Georgia and eat peas and vegetables'. This remark was greeted by bursts of laughter from the paratroopers who were in very high spirits. 'Don't worry, Boss, with the 101st, everything will go well !'. A tall man, his face as black as coal, even went as far as patting the general's back. 'If you're unemployed after the war, come over to see me at my Texas ranch. There'll always be a job for you !'* The paratrooper standing to attention carries a spoon in the side pocket of his M36 sack, the only piece of cutlery allowed by regulations.

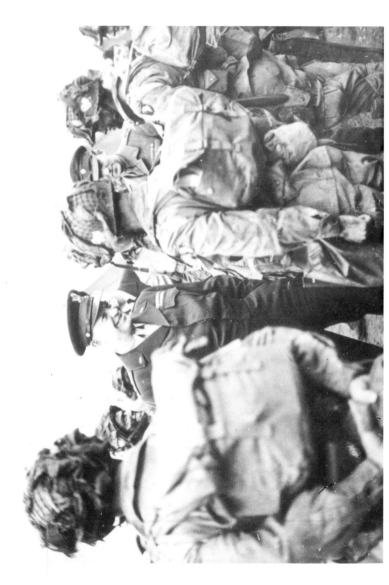

*Overleaf/*When compared with our cover photograph, this original document show how well our re-enactment teams worked. Nothing distinguished Lieutenant Kelso Horne from any private, when he was photographed at Saint Sauveur le Vicomte some time during the Normandy operation. Kelso's MIC steel helmet is cocked and worn over a small wool cap. The thin meshcamouflage netting has green and brown 'British made' hessian strips. The chin-straps of the steel shell are stuck through the netting, an usual practice among GIs. The 48-star flag appears on the right upper sleeve above the elbow reinforcement. The large cargo pockets, crammed to the point of bursting, are secured with straps. Many American officers preferred the Garand M1 rifle to the regulation issue US M1 carbine. A fragmenation grenade and a Colt pistol complete the armament. The thin chain of the whistle carried in the breast pocket is secured under the left shoulder strap. The water bottle is placed in a cloth cover on current issue to paratroopers. Although this picture has been 'staged' by the photographer, it conveys the tired appearance of the soldier, the stubble on his unshaved chin and his crumpled jacket.

THE US PARATROOPER OF D-DAY

'OK*, let's go!'* At 4:15 am, this Monday June 5, 1944, during a final general staff conference, Eisenhower confirmed his decision: Tuesday June 6 would be D-Day.

Probably never before in military history, had a General shouldered such a heavy responsibility. In the evening, Ike made an unformal inspection of the men who, in a few hours, would drop from the sky and face the German army, still very dangerous in spite of its recent setbacks. A lot has been achieved by the Americans since the pioneering days of 1941 when the US Army was making desperate efforts to emulate the German 'Fallschirmjäger' by creating its own airborne forces.

Origins and Evolution of US Paratrooper Units

It is now almost certain the development of the US Airborne troops evolved from the spectacular results obtained by the German paratroopers during the 1940 Western campaign. Although US military officials were unconcerned at that time, many felt that sooner or later their country would be drawn into the war and, under the impulse of a dauntless and energetic officer, Major-General W.C. 'Bill' Lee (later

nicknamed 'the father of the US paratroopers'), an airborne test batallion was raised at Fort Benning, Georgia, in July 1940. The start was promising and soon, the first US airborne unit came into being. Known as the 501st paratrooper battalion, the unit numbered 500 officers and enlisted men. Volunteers flocked to the new force and soon, regiments were formed and given numbers from 500 upp. Unlike contemporary German paratroops units, American airborne regiments did not answer to the air force but were controlled by the ground forces and used the same terminology. The first two US Airborne divisions, the 82nd and the 101st originated as infantry divisions which were named Airborne (A/B) in August 1942. In november 1941, during the Allied landing in North Africa, US paratroopers made their first operational jump when the 2nd Battalion of the 503rd P.I.R. commanded by the Lieutenant-Colonel Edson D. Raff was dropped near Oran. In July 1943, the 82nd division 'All Americans' was operational and later participated in the landings in Sicily and Italy. But however important these operations may have been, they appeared insignificant in view of the major operation every Allied soldier was expecting: the landing on the north-western coast of Europe. To this effect, in November 1943, the 82nd A/B (with the exception of the 504th P.I.R. which (Page 21) did not arrive until May 1944 and was thus not included in the Overlord deployment) was transferred to Northern Ireland and later to England where it took part in many tactical exercises together with its sister unit, the 101st A/B 'Screaming Eagles'. Raised in the United States with veteran officers of the 82nd A/B, the 'Screaming Eagles' arrived in Great-Britain in September 1943. Since their formation in 1942 and up to 1944, the organization of the airborne divisions was modified several

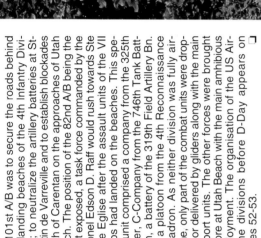

times on account of combat experience and the availability of air transportation. In 1942, the division comprised one paratrooper regiment and two glider regiment, totalling 8,505 men. In 1943, a new organizational chart boosted its strength to 12,979 men organised into two paratrooper and one glider regiment. In early 1944, however, this figures were reduced to 7,500 officers and men, resulting in support units being trimmed. The paratrooper regiments were now three with one two-battalion glider regiment.

The Missions of June 6

Numerous, well-documented publications focusing exclusively on the military operations are listed in the bibliography. They will enable researchers to follow the first events and the fluctuations of the battle hour after hour. The final plan, such as defined two weeks before D-Day after the latest intelligence reports had been submitted by French Resistance, attributed the following briefs to American airborne units:

- 82nd A/B was to seize the Ste-Mère-Eglise road junction; set-up bridgeheads west of town and across the marshy meadows; to hold off the German forces stationed in the zone of Pont l'Abbé-St-Sauveur le Vicomte; to open the way for the penetration towards the West coast of the peninsula.

- 101st A/B was to secure the roads behind the landing beaches of the 4th Infantry Division; to neutralize the artillery batteries at St-Martin de Varreville and to establish blockades North of Carentan on the approaches of Utah beach. The position of the 82nd A/B being the most exposed, a task force commanded by the Colonel Edson D. Raff would rush towards Ste Mère Eglise after the assault units of the VII Corps had landed on the beaches. This special unit comprised a company from the 325th Glider, C-Company from the 746th Tank Battalion, a battery of the 319th Field Artillery Bn. and a platoon from the 4th Reconnaissance Squadron. As neither division was fully airborne, only part of the combat units were dropped or delivered by gliders along with the main support units. The other forces were brought ashore at Utah Beach with the main amhibious deployment. The organisation of the US Airborne divisions before D-Day appears on pages 52-53.

The US Paratrooper of D-Day

Above: Based on a famous wartime document, the picture depicts 'All American' paras proudly displaying a trophy they have captured from the enemy. This photo shows the wide variety of uniforms and the different ways American paratroopers carried their equipment and armament. The presence of a glider pilot (with USAAF shoulder patch) at right is noteworthy. He probably insisted to pose with his comrades-at-arms before returning to Great Britain. The paratrooper in the centre, holding the flag soon had the opportunity to use the British Hawkins mine which is now innocuously strapped to his right calf. The other paratrooper holding the flag probably accounted for a 'Jerry' during the night as he is wearing the latter's belt. (re-enactment photograph).

Left: Although not a fiery mustang, this nag reminds those soldiers from Texas or Arizona of the horses back home. Some 1944 photographs show that US soldiers did not hesitate to ride draught horses - sometimes captured from the ennemy - when jeeps were were not available. (re-enactment photograph)

Right: Gathered by a cottage, these paratroopers enjoy a short break before going back to combat. They will soon link up with Task Force Raff coming in from the beachheads. (re-enactment photograph)

Pathfinders of 502nd P.I.R./82nd Airborne before taking off. How many of these men will live to see the 'Statue of Liberty' again? Nobody holds the answer but what is known is that paratrooper Devonchuk was not among them: he was one of the few killed on June 6 in a Ste-Mère Eglise street. This remarkable document provides many interesting details on US uniforms and equipment: additional camouflage was obtained by spraying or brushing the jump suits with green or brown paint; the unusual position of the M3 dagger strapped on the forearm of the fifth paratrooper at the right; the shoulder felt padding worn under the harness straps to avoid bruises caused by the weight of the equipment. Such paddings are worn by Robert M. Murphy who became famous for touching down in the garden of Mme Levrault, a primary school teacher in Ste-Mère Eglise. A wide diversity of make-up can be observed on the faces of the men: non-existant in some cases, black polish make some soldiers look like native Africans. This is probably the origin of the long-lasting myth of negro paratroopers which has lingered to the present day! In the foreground, the crew of the C-47 is kneeling at the front of their C-47 transport aircraft. The number chalked on the fuselage for the operation is noteworthy.

'La Fayette, here we come!'

The inhabitants of the Cotentin peninsula in Normandy were in for a major disappointment as they had expected that their liberators would arrive in the heat of a glorious day, with banners flying and bugles blowing. Instead, freedom came out of pitch black night. The liberators swooped in with stealthily, only to be seen surging from behind a hedgerow in the silence of their Goodyear rubber soles.

The 'Yanks' were back, almost 27 years to the day after the first American elements had landed in France on June 13, 1917. But this time they would use their full might to liberate the old continent which was then almost totally enslaved by Nazi Germany.

The spearhead of this powerful army, which was built in less than three years was formed by the airborne units. The paras paved the way for the troops coming in from the sea. In this night of freedom, thousands of soldiers were riding the grey waves of the Channel in the largest assault fleet the world has ever seen. However, the first contact between US troops and the French population was not always amicable. On many occasions, civilians were theatened by Americans paras who pointed their weapons at them. Near Sainte-Marie-du-Mont, liberation turned to drama when a young Frenchman was shot under the very eyes of his family by paratroopers who

had been ordered to 'shoot on sight'. But the enemy was also responsible for his share of horror: in a modest cottage, at a place named La Barquette, three children were doused with petrol and set alight by a German soldier who was incensed by the defeat of the Reich. Although assessing civilian casualties of June 6 is an impossible task, records show that the Calvados holds the unveiable record of deaths and ruins,

closely followed by the Manche department which also paid a heavy tribute to the liberation of France. At the end of the battle of Normandy, casualties amounted to more than 15,000 killed and 280,000 casualties out of 480,000 people. In addition, 60,000 buildings had been wrecked, and the cities of Périers, Saint-Lô, Montebourg, and Valognes had practically been laid waste.

ETUDIEZ LES PARACHUTISTES ALLIES
ILS SERONT PEUT-ÊTRE L'AVANT-GARDE DE LA
LIBÉRATION DANS VOTRE RÉGION

Above: Although the new American uniform had been widely shown in many contemporary publications and newsreels, many French people still expected the Americans to look like they did in 1917, with large 'boy-scout' hats and tight fitting tunics.

Right: Although millions of these leaflets were dropped over Normandy before D-Day, they failed to reach their purpose. Many people in France were confused by the appearance of their liberators. The sample shown here was found in the Les Mureaux area near Paris. Whether these leaflets were also dropped over Normandy is unknown. Any further information on this matter is welcome.

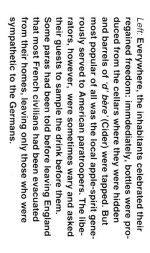

Left: Everywhere, the inhabitants celebrated their regained freedom: immediately, bottles were produced from the cellars where they were hidden and barrels of '*d' bère*' (Cider) were tapped. But most popular of all was the local apple-spirit generously served to American paratroopers. The liberators, however, were sometimes wary and asked their guests to sample the drink before them. Some paras had been told before leaving England that most French civilians had been evacuated from their homes, leaving only those who were sympathetic to the Germans.

Below: 'The Americans have arrived!' At dawn of June 6, the rumours became true, bringing forth a tremendous outbreak of joy among the inhabitants who warmly greeted the paratroopers, like those seen here taking a break in the hamlet of Ecoqueneauville. Note the wide felt or heavy canvas padding placed on the shoulders under the straps, of the second man from right.

Above: 'How to find one's way about in these damned hedgerows, they all look the same and are almost never reported on the maps?' This seems to be the concern of those paratroopers of the 82nd Airborne Division. Note the general issue plastic wrist compass on the waist belt of the man at left; and, the dog-tags, metal individual identification plates, worn around the neck. In case of death, one of the plates is taken away by the burial officials while the other one is left on the body for any further identification. (re-enactment photograph)

Above: Wearing the typical blurred camouflage blouse issued to German panzergrenadiers and sharpshooters, this sniper is being frisked by an officer of the 82nd A/B. Skilfully hidden in high trees or lurking in church steeples, German snipers preferably picked off officers whom they easily identified through their equipment (map cases or binoculars). Resultingly, American officers soon decided to look like privates, keeping the tell-tale accessories out of sight, and carrying a Garand M1 rifle like enlisted personnel.

Below: 'Where is your infantry?' A question German officers frequently asked their American captors. Highly motorised, the US Army had huge quantities of vehicles and from the dawn of June 6, the first gliders were delivering the ubiquitous jeeps. The vehicle shown here sports the markings of the 504th P.I.R., a unit recently ferried from Italy and which did not take part in D-Day operations. This jeep might possibly have been handed over at the last minute by this regiment to another unit of the 82nd A/B.

MYTHS DIE HARD.

Five decades later, the saga of US paratroopers is still shrouded in myths!

The First Liberated Town.

Ste-Mère Eglise is purported to be the first French town liberated by the Allies. In fact, it was the city of Ranville, East of the Orne river, which was first liberated by British paratroopers of the 13th (Lancashire) Battalion, the Parachute Regiment on June 6 at 2.30 a.m. It is also widely believed that US paratroopers were slaughtered while fighting in the streets of Ste-Mère Eglise. This myth was fostered by the movie 'The Longest Day'. These facts do not resist a close scrutiny: in fact, the little city was totally evacuated during the night and without engagement by the Flak support company stationed there. Around 4.30 a.m., Lieutenant Colonel Edward 'Cannonball' Krause, commanding officer of the 505th P.I.R. 3rd battalion entered the city with 160 men amidst sporadic gunfire. In all, some 15 US paratroopers were killed or wounded in the streets of Ste-Mère Eglise on 6 June.

□

Left: The face of this paratrooper shows traces of strain: he has had no rest since dawn. His standard infantry equipment consists of cartridge-belt, water bottle and first-aid kit. The large pouch pockets of the jacket show their usefulness: crammed with spare socks, batteries, D-rations, spoon, razor, soap, weapon cleaning-kit and of course cigarettes and sweets. (re-enactment photograph).

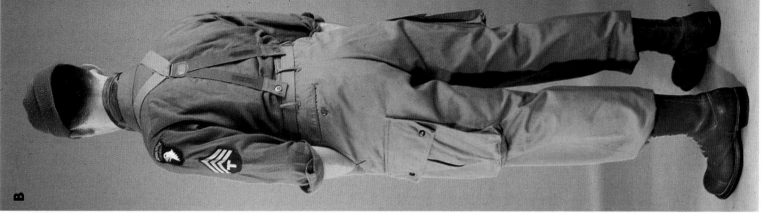

After the specification and issue of the infantry new field uniform, comprising the famous M 1941 field jacket, the Quartermaster Corps undertook the examination of special uniforms upon request of some army corps unsatisfied with existing model.

The Airborne units required a completely different uniform, better suited to their missions. The main criticism was the lack of large cargo pockets on the woollen jacket and trousers.

The obsessive individualism which typifies some 'elite' corps led to the introduction of a specific uniform. In addition, the trend in the Quartermaster Corps favoured the issue of special clothing designed for specific combat situation, such as the ground configuration, climate etc. The paratroopers had things their way: after a jump overall, practical in training but inadequate for combat operations, was rejected in 1941, a new experimental two-piece uniform was presented to the officials of the future airborne units. After slight modifications, particularly dealing with the fastening of the pockets, the final design was approved in December 1941, leading to the specification of the jump jacket designated as 'Coat, Parachute jumper'. In early 1942, the trousers were approved, specified and designated as trousers, parachute jumper (this set, jacket and trousers will be better known as jump-suit M-1942)

Below: 1943 at Camp McDonald, North Carolina: two paras pose proudly for the camera. Each man wears an immaculate jump jacket. At left, Private Porcella who gave us precious details about American paras, sports his airborne qualification badge above the left chest pocket.

AIRBORNE UNIFORM

The Jump Jacket.

Manufactured in beige cotton poplin, the coat parachute jumper looked like a four-pocket tunic gathered around the waist. There was no lining. The pockets gave the garment its typical outline; they were expandable and adjusted to the contents by means of vertical bellows. An extension was possible thanks to four pressure studs placed on the pocket, and two press-sockets located at the corners of the asymmetrical flaps.

Above: These two paratroopers kindly display every detail of their M1942 brand new uniform. A. The 4th grade Technician from the 101st A/B is wearing the USAAF mechanic's woolknit cap, a small, non-regulation headgear which sometimes replaced the knitted M-1941 beanie. Note the typical trousers bellow-shaped pockets. The woollen shirt is standard issue, and the scarf was madet from parachute material. B. This view clearly shows the baggy appearance of the trousers worn above the brand new jump boots. Suspenders were insdispensable when the trousers were overloaded with numerous equipments crammed in the cargo pockets.

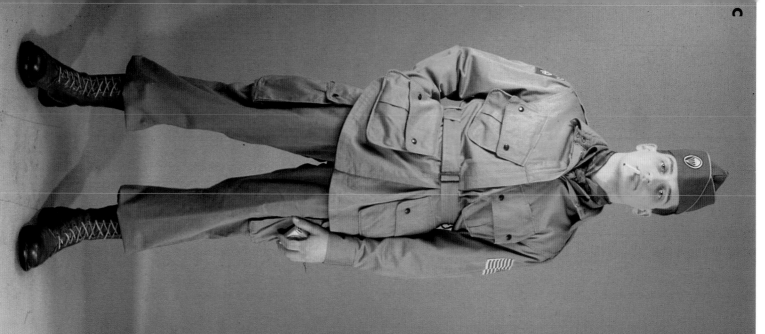

C

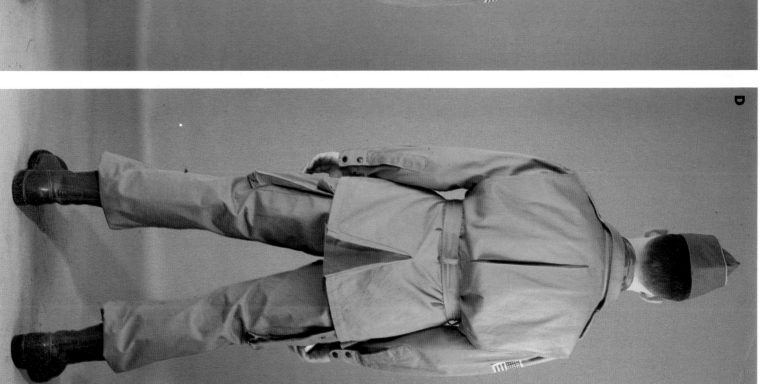

D

Above:

C. This 82nd A/B private wears with satisfaction a mint uniform he has just obtained from 'supply'. The different shades between the jacket and the trousers colors are due to the different dye solutions used by the various manufacturers. These two garments have never been worn and show their original color. A little multiple-use fob pocket can be seen half way from the upper pocket can be seen: it may contain a pencil, the safety lever of a hand-grenade or the hook of the TL 122 angle-head flashlight. D Comfort pleats can be seen here in the back and the bottom of the jacket. The use of pressure studs on the collar and cuffs is typical. The shoulder straps are secured near the collar by a pressure stud.

The Jump Trouser.

Cut in the same material as the jacket, the

According to the manufacturers, the two breast pockets were slightly slanted for better access. The jacket sealed with a front with a metal zip-fastener under flap, and a light canvas belt with metal buckle. At the top of the closing under flap there is a small vertical pocket sealing with flap by two zip-fasteners and holding the M2 folding knife. Full freedom of movements was provided by three pleats in the back: two running from the shoulder to the waist and one placed in the cen-ter, pinched at the waist and running all the way down. This jacket was worn over the regular wool shirt and possibly with the highneck sweater.

Trousers, Parachute Jumper had the same pur-pose, i.e. a to be practicable with two large hold-all cargo pockets on the thighs and running down to the knees. The manufacturing features were also identical, bellows, asymmetrical flaps sea-ling with pressure studs: two on the flap and four on the pocket. In addition to these large cargo pockets, there was a small fob pocket on the right breast, two pockets slightly slanting and two fla-pless back pockets; the left one sealing with a small bakelite button identical to those of the fly and suspenders. The tailored trousers were sligh-tly tapered around the ankles so as to fit neatly into the boot. The lining of the pockets and the inner reinforcements were, as for the pink trou-sers in white cotton fabric.

17

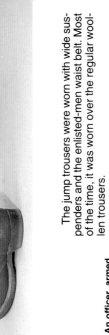

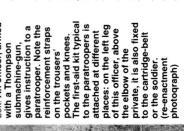

The jump trousers were worn with wide suspenders and the enlisted-men waist belt. Most of the time, it was worn over the regular woollen trousers.

A Fragile Uniform.

Immediately set to production, the new uniform passed its 'trial by fire' in November 1942 during Operation 'Torch' in North Africa. If the practical side of it is undeniable, the assembly jacket-trousers which is cut, let us remember in light poplin quickly turns out much too fragile for the missions assigned to airborne units. The knees and the elbows were prematurely worn out and the large pouch pocket filled with numerous accessories were quickly torn away. Therefore, at the end of 1943, when the paratroopers of the 82nd A/B are stationed in Britain after their tour on the Mediterranean theater of operation, arrangements were made to

Left: An officer, armed with a Thompson submachine-gun, gives instruction to a paratrooper. Note the reinforcement straps on the trousers' pockets and knees. The first-aid kit typical to the paratroopers is attached at different places: on the left leg of this officer, above the elbow of the private, it is also fixed to the cartridge-belt or to the soldier. (re-enactment photograph)

Above: This magnificient jump jacket, a genuine D-Day relic, comes from the Montebourg area. The two-tone camouflage pattern applied with a brush breaks efficiently the original beige color which proved inadequate for operations in Normandy. This practice was particularly popular among pathfinders. The gas-detection armband was still in place when the garment was found. The lower pockets and the elbows (not visible here) are reinforced. This jacket has been subjected to anti-gas treatment resulting in a clammy, unpleasant touch. It has also been crudely camouflaged with paint. The name of the paratrooper 'Reodon' is written on an improvised strip rarely used in army ground forces at the time. The shoulder sleeve insignia of the 101st A/B has been removed, leaving its darker imprint on the faded cloth. The first sergeant stripes also received their share of camouflage paint.

improve the uniforms. At that stage, the M-1943 all-units outfit was not yet on regular supply and the M1942 assembly had to be reinforced.

The Reinforced Jump Uniform

Careful study of some original photographs taken during the Normandy campaign shows that in most cases, US paratroopers were dressed with reinforced uniforms. These reinforcements were placed at the elbows of the jacket and the bellows of the lower pockets; on the trousers, they were placed at the most exposed spots: the knees and the bellows of the large pockets. Two straps used to secure the stuffed pockets were slipped in the inside-leg seam or just sewn flat over a few centimeters. The reinforcements were cut in heavy canvas obtained from old equipment: duffel-bags or shelter canvas. Their color varied

from dirty grey to dark olive-drab. Today, nothing allows to ascertain where and when the jump uniforms have been reinforced. The study of 'surviving' uniforms shows that these reinforcements were added after their manufacture. The trousers legs and the jacket sleeves have been unstitched in order to slip in reinforcements pieces and restitched using a different thread. In most cases, this work has been crudely made. To establish the time when these modifications were made, pictures show paratroopers in training in the USA and in Britain in March/April 1944 wearing non-reinforced uniforms. One might conclude that these modifications have been enforced just before June 5, probably by the salvage shops or subcontracted to British manufacturers

Although many uniforms were reinforced just before D-day, the original mint uniform as shown has also been worn. Whether reinfor-

ced or not, after weeks in combat, the jump suits were in such a pitiful condition that they had to be withdrawn from the troops and replaced with brand new outfits prior to their return to Britain. (testimony Tom Porcella 508th PIR ▢

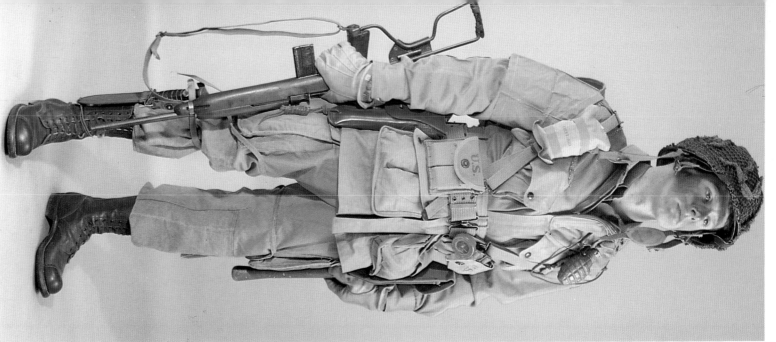

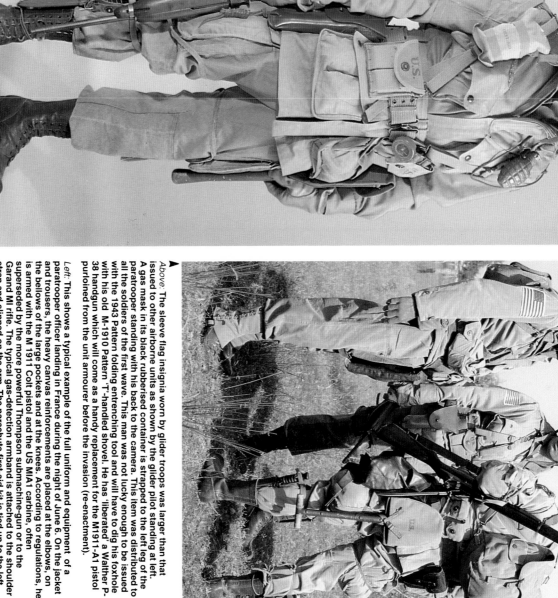

Above: The sleeve flag insignia worn by glider troops was larger than that issued to other airborne units as shown by the glider pilot standing at left. A gas mask in its black rubberised container is strapped to the left leg of the paratrooper standing with his back to the camera. This item was distributed to all the soldiers of the first wave. This man was not lucky enough to be issued with the 1943 Pattern folding entrenching tool and will have to dig his foxhole with his old M-1910 Pattern 'T-handled shovel. He has 'liberated' a Walther P-38 handgun which will come as a handy replacement for the M1911-A1 pistol purloined from the unit armourer before the invasion (re-enactment).

Left: This shows a typical example of the full uniform and equipment of a paratrooper officer landing in France during the night of June 6. On the jacket and trousers, the heavy canvas reinforcements are placed at the elbows, on the bellows of the large pockets and at the knees. According to regulations, he is armed with the M1911 Colt pistol and the US M1A1 carbine, often superseded by the more powerful Thompson submachine-gun or to the Garand M1 rifle. The typical gas-detection armband is attached to the shoulder strap and slipped on the arm. The parachute first-aid kit is tied up to the left strap of the harness. This officer carries the same equipment as the men : foldable entrenching tool M 1943, the rucksack and the M 1936 lashing with rectangular ammunition pouch made in England for the Airborne units. No rank insignias can be seen either on the shoulder straps nor helmet. It probably denotes the suspicion of this officer towards the snipers, from experience gained in Italy.

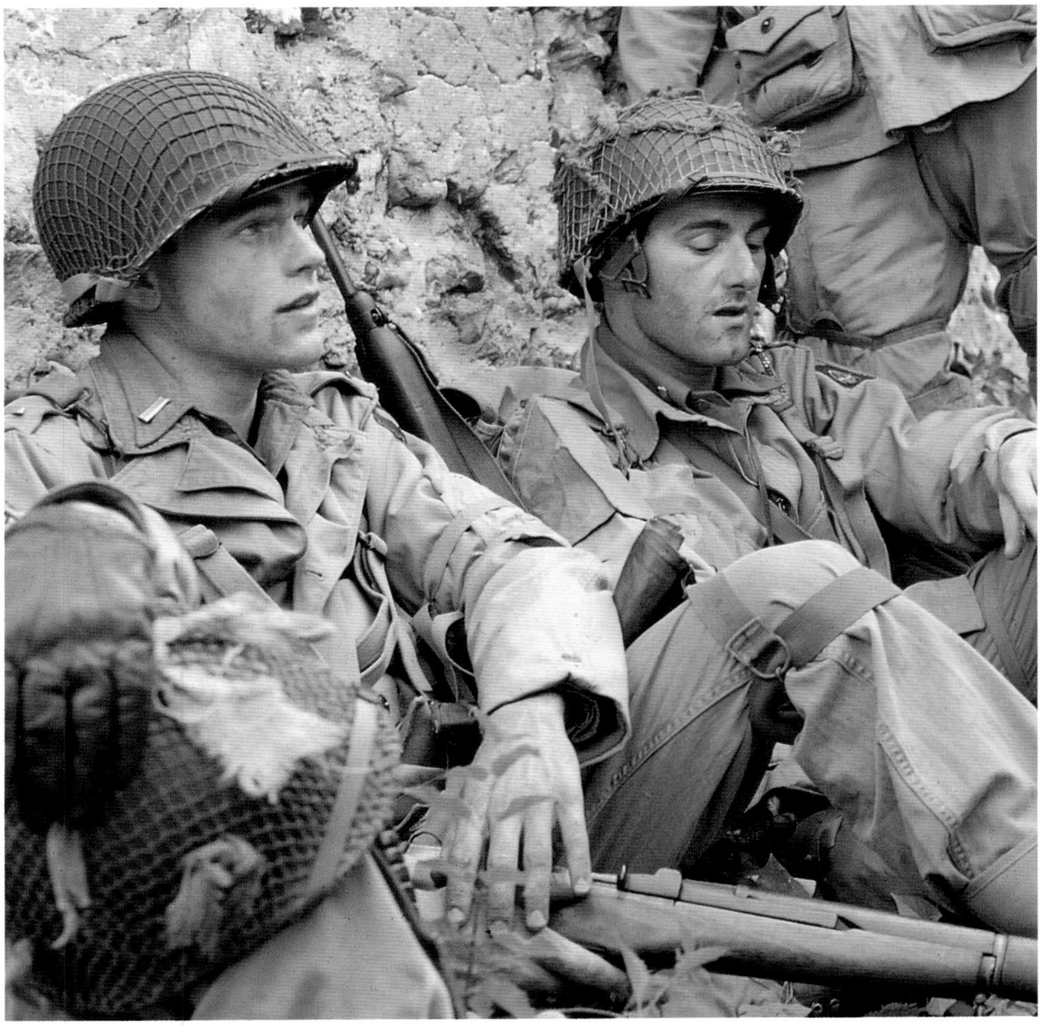

THE M1C STEEL HELMET

The M1C steel helmet is a conversion of the MI steel helmet developed for the Airborne units.

Like the MI, the M1C helmet consists of two components: a liner and a steel shell. The liner is manufactured from a lightweight compressed fibre and is similar to the standard army issue model. However, it includes an additional 'V' shaped neckstrap riveted to each side of the liner, the two ELEMENTS of which are reinforced half-way up by a cross strap. At the top of the 'V' is a metal buckle (in brass or blackened steel) with single tang on which a leather-embossed chin cup is clipped. A wash-leather type skin is glued on the inner side. This assembly ensures the stability of the helmet on the wearer's head, this being essential to the paratrooper, subject to violent shocks. (air-stream under the helmet during the jump or at the parachute opening). On the ground, this chinstrap is useless and therefore stuck under the straps of the liner, the 'V' shaped chinstrap being folded back inside. The steel shell is also of standard army issue with the exception of the chin-strap. The regular chinstrap is modified by adding a press-stud fastener strap to be inserted into a socket riveted inside the liner holding the assembly together. The examination of wartime photographs and contemporary helmets shows than numerous MIC steel shells had half-circle chin-strap attachment rings. These special devices appear to be specific to the M1C helmets. However, standard rectangular chin-strap fittings were also seen. However, in the field these fixed attachments proved fragile and were replaced at the end of 1943 with mobile rectangular rings welded to a hinge in the helmet.

Helmet Markings

In addition to the well-known markings of the M.P.'s and medics, a complete set of tactical signs appeared on the helmets of the 101st Airborne. Specific to the 101st A/B, this scheme resulted from a Headquarters Conference held two weeks before D-Day. The officials of this division never exposed to combat were concerned about develop a way of identifying on the spot the unit of any paratrooper reaching the ground. It was then suggested to paint on the side of the helmet a sign easy to memorize: the four aces of playing cards and simple shapes. With the approval of the division commanding officer, General Maxwell D. Taylor, this project was immediately launched. These insignias were about 4.5 cm high and painted in white on both sides of the helmet. The meaning of these marking has been retraced thanks to the testimony of the Major-General G.J. Higgings, Chief of Staff of the 101st Airborne division who attended this conference in 1944.

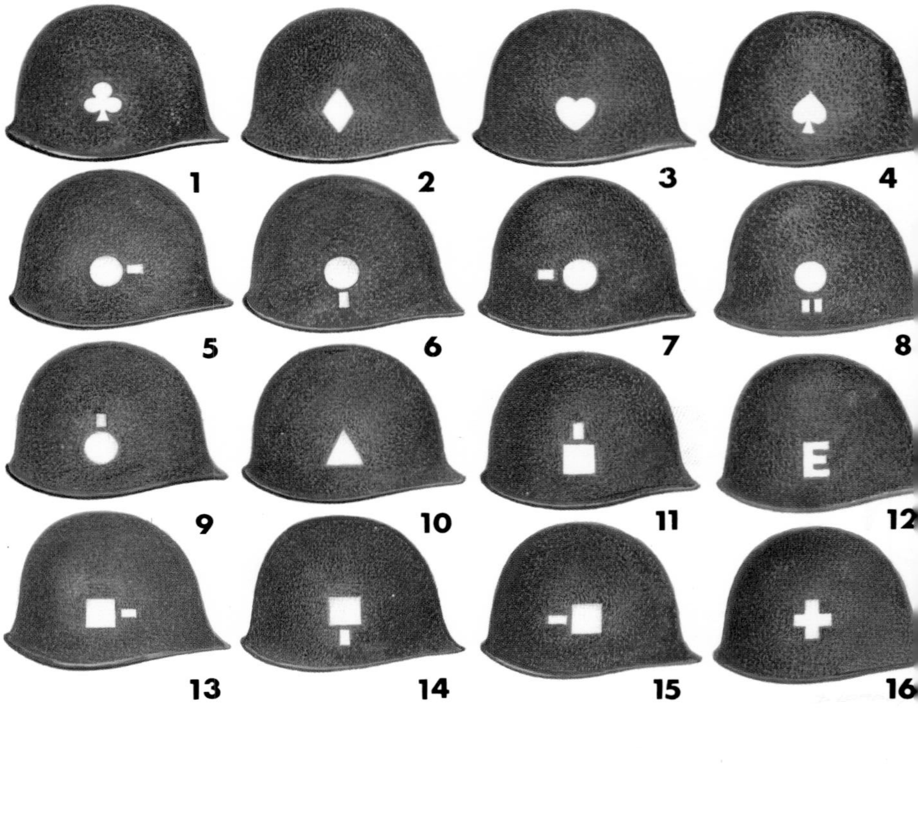

101st AIRBORNE DIVISION HELMET MARKINGS

The position of the white bar/dot symbols indicates: HQ: bar above the dot. Right: 1st Battalion; below: 2nd Battalion and left: 3rd Battalion.

1. 327 th Glider Inf. Regt. 2. 501st P.I.R. 3. 502nd P.I.R. 4. 506th P.I.R.

5. 321 st Glider Field Artillery Bn. 6. 377th Parachute Field Artillery Bn. 7. 907th Glider Field Artillery Bn. 8. 463rd Parachute Field Artillery Bn.

9. HQ. Divisional Artillery. 10. 81st A.A.A. Bn. 11. 101st Divisional Reconnaissance Plat. 12. 326th Engineer Bn.

13. 101st Divisional Signal Coy. 14. 426th QMC Coy. 15. 801st Ordnance Coy. 16. 326th Medic Coy

(Drawings: Daniel Lordey, from a study by Cameron Laughlin published by AMI magazine)

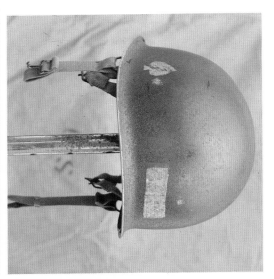

Left: The glider pilot at left wears the regular M1 helmet. Note the typical way of wearing the M1941 field jacket over the herringbone twill overall. The silver bars of First-Lieutenant are pinned to the jacket shoulder straps and on the left collar tab. The winged-propeller of the USAAF is pinned to the right collar tab.

Overall view of a complete MIC steel helmet showing the features of the special chin-strap of the liner. Three variations of the leather chin-cups only used in June 1944 are shown at right. The survival D ration is described in the 'equipment' section.

Recovered from the actual combat zones, these two exceptional pieces display the particularities of the M1C steel helmet particularly the half-circle chin-strap fixation rings.

At left, the ace of spades indicates the 506th P.I.R. of the 101st A/B. The white dot indicates the 1st battalion, the unit of NCO Atlee killed at Saint-Côme-du-Mont and resting at the Saint-Laurent-sur-Mer cemetery. The white horizontal stripe painted on the back of the helmet denotes an NCO while the officers' had a vertical stripe.

The steel helmet at right is coming from the Carentan area and belonged to a Medical Corps NCO. There were many size variations in the painting of the red crosses. The white bakground could be round or square. This symbol was applied between one and four times around the helmet either crudely or finely made.

Right:
Detail of the chin strap system showing the press-stud fastener of the webbing strap securing the steel-shell to the liner. The fixation of the chin-strap is of standard rectangular type.

Far right: Detail of the chin-strap fitting on the steel-shell. The 'D' ring was only used on MIC helmets. This type is shown on the color wartime document printed on page 27.

THE JUMP BOOTS

From 1940, following some experiences carried-out at Fort Benning by the test platoon, the QMC infantry board in charge of the new Airborne equipments decided that the jump boots were the major component of the jump uniform. Two types of boots were examined. First, the laced boots with rubber soles of German paratroopers and then, those with a top reinforcement tongue used by the US Forest Service firemen. Several prototypes using the best features of these boots were manufactured and tested by the 501st Parachute Battalion and the 502nd P.I.R. between January 1941 and July 1942. Numerous alterations took place before the design was approved on 2 August 1942 (Designated : Boots, Parachute Jumper (Quartermaster specification B.Q.D. N°58B 3 August 1942). This specification is established by the Boston Quartermaster Depot (B.Q.D.) responsible for the design of all Army footwear. Although these jump boots were only designed for paratroopers, they were sometimes worn by soldiers of the glider units by 'esprit de corps' as they too, were airborne.

Far right: This advertisement uses the prestige of the paratrooper jump boot to promote the civilian production of Roblee, brand name of the Brown Shoe Co. This advertisement emphasizes the protection features of the boot: the reinforcements of the heel and over the toes, the bevelled heel and the rounded sole edges.

Right: The stance of this officer shows the details of the parachute jumper boots, particularly the lacing method without knot at the top of the boot leg. Maintained by a webbing strap, the M3 dagger is simply slipped into the jump boot. The crossed rifles pinned on the collar of the shirt indicate the infantry, service branch of the paratroopers.
(re-enactment)

Below: **A.B.** A superb pair of boots of the famous maker Corcoran, supplier of the wealthy paratroopers. Note the maker's cloth label and the hole ornaments on the toe cap seam. This model contains 12 pairs of eyelets.

C.D. These boots have been manufactured by a civilian contractor of the US Army, the International Shoe Co., as indicated by the markings ink-stamped at the top of the leg.

Roblee

SHOES FOR MEN

Shoes for Men of America

$600 to $800

Description.

The new shoes have a high leg and are manufactured in brown chromed-tanned leather. They have 12 pairs of eyelets (11 or 13 on some variations). The tongue placed under the lacing is sewn on the top of the leg. It is reinforced at the back by an overstitched strap. The toe cap is very strong and deeply curved giving to the jump boot its familiar 'bean-shape' silhouette. The ankle is protected by a heavy canvas band sewn inside the shoe and showing outside two, three or even four diagonal seams. The non-slip patterned sole is in black rubber and assembled by a double stitching and hobnails. The front-bevelled heel is cut from the same material and the honeycombing around it creates a shock-absorbing effect. The laces are in brown cotton or natural leather. The 1943 Quartermaster catalog shows the availability of the Boots, Parachute Jumper in 119 different sizes (stock No. 72-B-217 to 72-B-336-20).

Markings.

The shoe size is printed in the leather sole just above the heel. It is also shown inside the leg with the maker's logo, the date and references of the contract, either stamped in black ink or embossed in the leather when made by the famous manufacturer 'Corcoran'. The paratroopers were very fond of their boots and although, by regulations, these were solely reserved for combat, they would be worn with all others uniforms. The bottom of the trousers are always tucked into the top of the boot showing clearly the full boot and allowing it to distinguish at first sight a paratrooper from the other troopers, still wearing their old canvas leggings'.

Below: **Detail of the soles with bevelled heel and the non-slip pattern. The size is printed in the leather, 7C on the left and 8D on the Corcoran boots on the right, having the 'C' of their brand name moulded into the heel. In many cases, the logo of the main US rubber manufacturers appear on the heel.**

'Boots through the air with the greatest protection!'

First in Sicily, hours before landing barges. First in Italy, were our paratroopers. Landing via chute is like jumping from a fifteen-foot height. An instep "bumper" protects the arch, and toes are extra reinforced. And note wedge heel and rounded sole, so no slivering catches as wearer jumps. The makers of Roblee have made literally thousands of dozens of these U.S. paratrooper boots.

Left: At this English base at Saltby, the Red Devils of the 508th Parachute Infantry Regiment (82nd A/B) concentrate on the final check of their T-5 parachute prior to their jump over France. Hastily sewn on the gas detection armband, the US 48-star national flag is already partially torn away on the man at the left.

Right: The evening of 5 June, at their base at Exeter, the 'Screaming Eagles' of the 3rd battalion, 506th P.I.R. (101st A/B) are ready to board their respective C-47s. The dismantled rifles are carried on the er in their carrying cases, the other equipment being placed s convenience.
The third man from the left is wearingat the bearer his Colt .45 cal. holster on the left side of the belt, an unusual practice in the US Army. The C-47s in the background is the leader aircraft of the 440th Troop Carrier Group, 98th Squadron and the radome of the SCR. 717 radar can be seen under the fuselage.

The morale of those paratroopers smiling to the photographer is in high spirit and the terrible tension suffered during those long waiting days finally vanished, '*This time, it's the good one, let's go !*' For those men under intensive training during months, it is like a gigantic spring of energy and violence which will at last be released. The time is over when scuffling in the pubs, throwing chairs and tables at Royal Marines and the sometimes fatal brawls with the negroes of the Quartermaster Corps: this time it is face to face with the German army, the most powerful force of all times, which brought to heel the major part of Europe. The struggle promised to be tough as this time, there will be no military policemen around to separate the fighters !

THE JUMP AND THE PARACHUTES

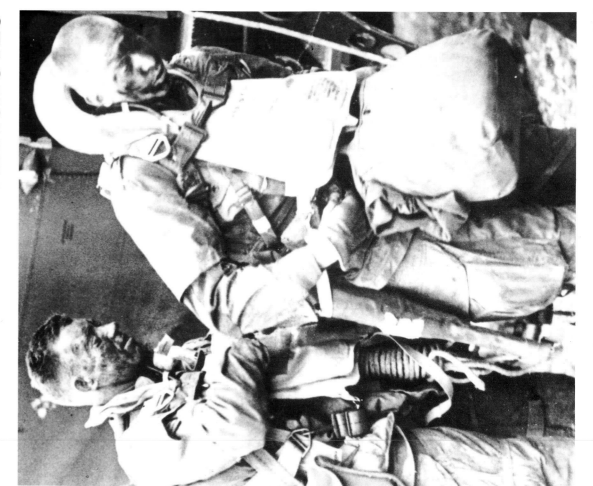

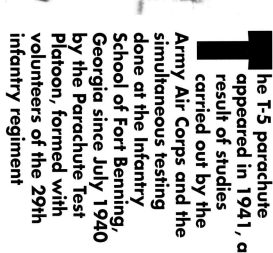

The T-5 parachute appeared in 1941, a result of studies carried out by the Army Air Corps and the simultaneous testing done at the Infantry School of Fort Benning, Georgia since July 1940 by the Parachute Test Platoon, formed with volunteers of the 29th infantry regiment

Far left: Donning of the T-5 parachute on the back of an officer armed with the USM1 A1 carbine in its carrying case attached to the pistol belt. More cumbersome than useful, the life preserver jacket is set in place : in case of coming down in flooded areas, the wearer must unhook the reserve parachute placed on it before being able to inflate it. This is almost impossible when the cotton webbings become tighter in contact with the water. An additional piece of clothing, probably a raincoat is rolled under the flap of the M1936 field bag.

Left: The assistance of a comrade is almost essential to put on the T-5 parachute after the fitting of the basic individual equipment. This document (place and unit unknown) shows the gas-detection armband, the special ammunition pouches loaded with hand-grenades on the soldier on the right or with magazines on the G.I. Ross who wrote his name on the flap of his M1936 field bag. Note the protective goggles on the helmet of the man on the right.

Although modern for that time, the T-5 parachute has a major defect: the locking-system of its harness. When a paratroor is dropped under ennemy fire or over flooded areas, it is vital for him to remove his parachute as fast as possible. On the T-5 model, there are no fewer than three snap-hooks (one at the sternum and two at the inside-leg) to release the harness. In addition, it is very difficult to reach these snap-hooks when burdened with the full combat equipment. This heavy deficiency was to cost many lives of US paratroopers who drowned in the swamps of the Merderet, captives of their own parachute. The only emergency solution to this was cutting the harness with a knife. This way of escaping is often confirmed by the visual examination of the T-5 harnesses, survivors of the landing in Normandy.

The reserve parachute (the ventral or chest-pack), although a 'luxury' reserved for US troops at the time (these were not in use by the British and the German paratroopers),has not been of a great help on 6 June, 1944. Most of the jumps were done from an altitude of 150m,allowing just the main parachute to open and slow the paratrooper's fall before reaching the ground.

THE T-5 PARACHUTE

The following descriptions mainly refer to the photograph showing the harness of the T-5 parachute on page 26 and also to the general views of pages 30-31.

The Canopy

The canopy is in nylon with small camouflaged khaki-greenish shade spots. Its superficy has about 52 m2 composed of 28 spindles. In the center, an opening of 0.44 m. diameter allows air to escape assuring a better stability during the jump. 28 rigging lines of 6.70 m. long spread around the canopy are attached to the 4 harness lifting devices (shown on page 26, **G** and **K**).

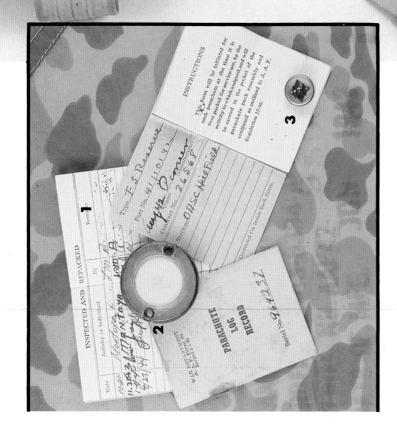

Above: On this T-5 parachute background are placed :
1 - Parachute maintenance booklet recording the number and date of the jumps and maintenance. On the opened sample, the last training jump has been done in Britain on 21 April, 1944.
2 - Phosphorescent signal disk. Stappled on the back or on any piece of equipment, its brightness allows, during a night march, to spot the preeceding man. It is also used to locate dropped equipment on the ground. 3. Tiny escape compass placed in the small pocket 20 described page 44.

Left: The reserve parachute (chest-pack), back of the shown the two hooks and the pocket holding the maintenance and folding booklet. On the left of the chest-pack are placed the climbing rope and on the right an English-French conversation manual which will prove useful to ask questions to the Norman farmers awaken in the middle of the night. The set is placed on a poster extolling the paratroopers' glory posted so as encourage the buying of war bonds.

Left: This striking propaganda photograph was taken in the United States in August 1943. The man in the foreground is equipped with an early-made T-5 parachute, noticeable by its white harness and unpainted buckles. Also note the absence of ringlets designed to hold the weapon case, normally placed at the level of the right shoulder. The half-circle chin strap fixation ring of the steel shell M1C early models, is noteworthy. The equipment of this paratrooper is restricted to the minimum : the compass pocket is partly hidden by the chest pack. (US Army)

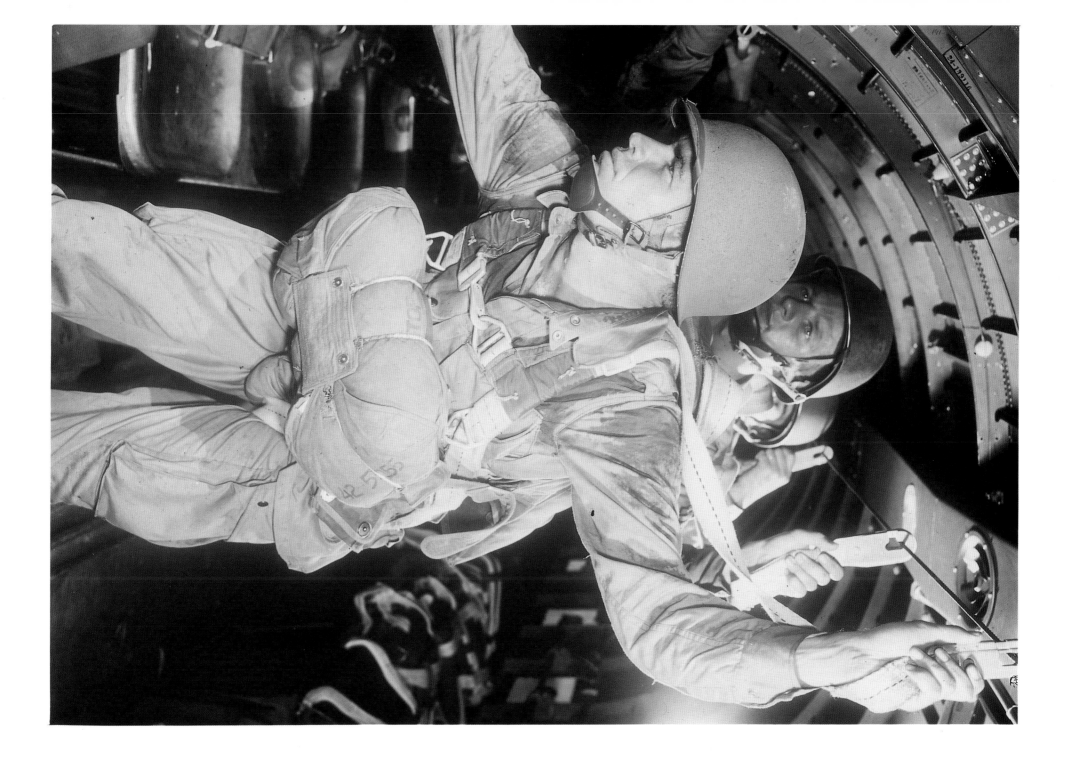

Right: Inside a C-47s at the base at Upottery, these men of the 506th P.I.R. (101st A/B) are briefed before the departure. The officer standing, his binoculars at the side, wears the escape scarf (map of Normandy printed on cotton) tied around his neck. An extra pocket has been added to the left sleeve. The green and brown strips placed in the netting of the helmet are British-made.

Below: On the evening of 5 June at the base of Upottery, these two men assist each other fitting their equipments. This excellent photograph shows the large variety in the issue and wear of equipment. The trooper at the left wears his entrenching tool on the right hip and received a padded case for his weapon. His comrade however carries his entrenching tool on the left side and his M1 rifle simply hangs on the chest by the sling. Note also the unusual presence of a submachine gun magazine pouch probably very useful to hold extra K rations. The M-5 gas mask is clearly visible under the main parachute.

The Jump and the Parachutes

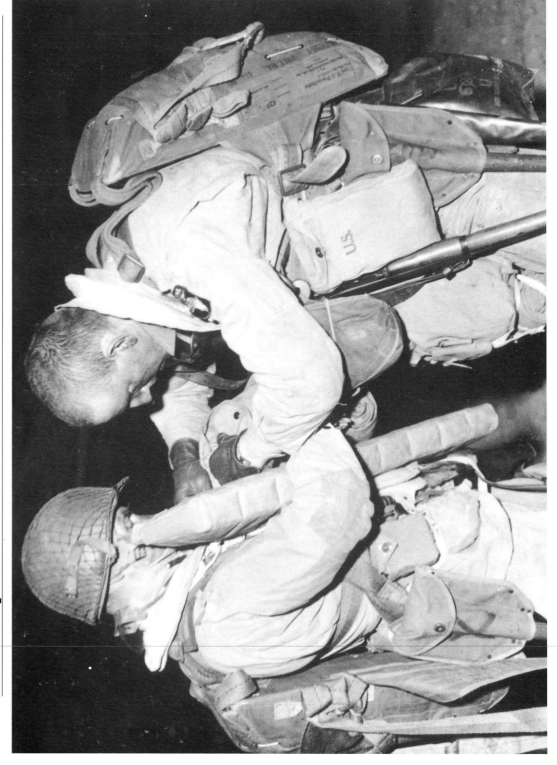

THE HARNESS (from page 26)

It consists of a very strong webbing strap assembly, white on the first models and khaki later on. It is secured on the chest by a snap-hook (1) placed on the main harness right strap and locking in a ringlet (2) located on the left brace. The 4 straps of the harness form a flattened 'V' with a kind of reinforced seat (3) at the base on which rests the buttocks of the paratrooper. From this seat two adjustables straps, the waders (4 and 5) are passing between the paratrooper's legs and are attached to the front of the harness (6 and 7) using the system described above : snap-hook + ringlet. Two 'D' shaped rings (8 and 9) placed in the middle of the harness front braces are used to fit onto the snap-hooks of the reserve parachute. A 'V' shape ring sewn at the level of the right shoulder (10) fits to the snap-hook of the padded case of the Garand rifle or any other equipment needed for the mission.

THE PARACHUTE PACK

The parachute pack contains the main parachute and is fixed on the harness with 4 cross-straps (a,b,c,d) acting as a back to the user. The pack-bag is strengthened by a metal frame; it consists of 4 flaps (page 31 back view) closing the sides of the pack; 24 eyelet-holes are spread on these 4 flaps. Two straps are

Left: The night has fallen this 5 June and the paratroopers of the 506th P.I.R. (I0Ist A/B) are boarding their respective C-47s. The men are overburdened by the incredible weight of their equipment well shown here, needing the help of the crew to climb inside. On the left, wearing a sweater and leggings, the pilot slipped on a Mae West and smokes a last cigarette before taking off.

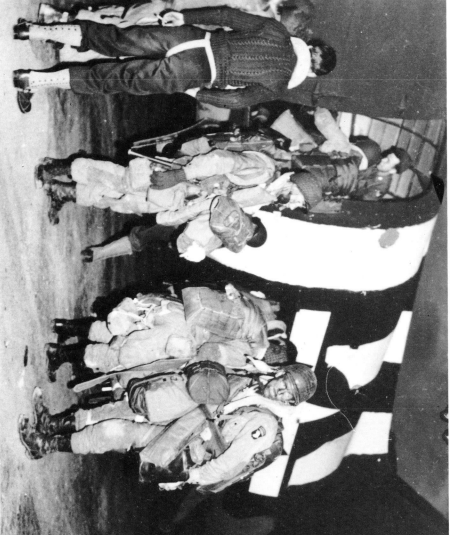

Right: Let's go for the biggest adventure of the century ! With a painful grimace caused by the effort, this paratrooper can hardly pull himself up into the fuselage of the Douglas C-47 8-Y of the 98th Squadron, 440th Troop Carrier Group. Including the 150 aircraft transferred to the British airborne troops, no less than 1,000 of this big twin-engined transport aircraft participated in the D-Day operations. The figure 'one' chalked near the door indicates a leading aircraft. The man is armed with the Thompson M1 submachine gun and the M3 trench knife with leather scabbard stapped to the leg. The complete history and all the technical details of the Douglas C-47 are exposed in the book of Yves Tariel : *'The History of the Douglas DC-3'* (civilian designation) published at the Editions Lavauzelle in 1985. Equipment well shown here, needing the help of the crew to climb inside.

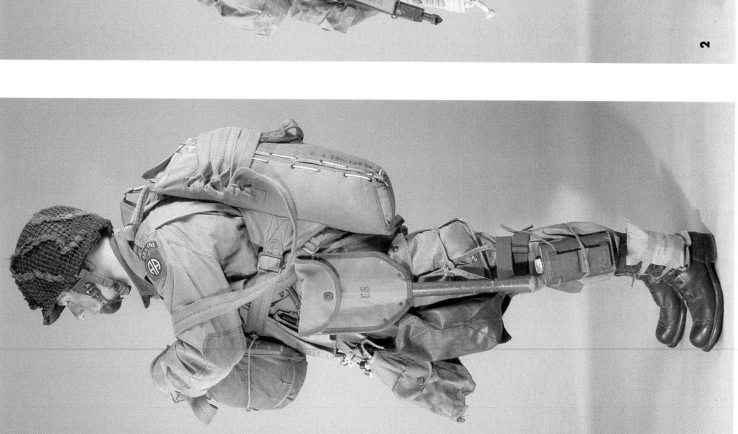

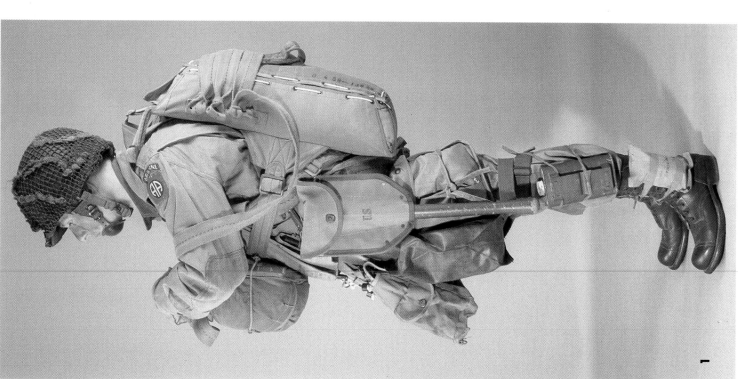

1. Static line passing above the arm (beware of under-the-arm-openings !). The entrenching tool M. 43 is used as well as the M. 1910 tool which is considered more dangerous during the jump, due to its T-shaped handle. The gas mask is placed in its tight rubber bag with one strap around the waist and another one around the leg. The Hawkins mine, which the paratrooper will quickly set on a practical target after reaching the ground, is strapped to on the calf. Below this, the first-aid package is fixed on the jump boot with its four thin straps.

2. The parachute harness is buckled over the life preserver vest which would interfere with its inflation if needed. However, the harness release is still possible. The M.36 musette-bag under the chest-pack is fixed to the suspenders; its outer flap faces the paratrooper's legs, covering the

closing buckles to avoid any entanglement during the opening of the parachute.

3. This back view clearly shows the reinforcement patches on the elbows and the large pouch pockets of the trousers. Note also the webbing straps holding the pockets.

4. This side shows :
- the 20 or 30-round magazine pouches for the Thompson MI submachine - gun (these made in Britain); - the coiled rope, very useful when landing in a tree or on a roof; - the M3 trench knife in its M8 scabbard. This one is secured to the calf with a strap recovered from an old M.1928 sack; - the Thompson MI submachine gun with shoulder sling fixed under the belt connecting the main and reserve parachutes.

sewn at the edge on each side of the metal frame : one at the right measures 90 cm (page 26, **E**) and one at the left 15.5 cm is fitted with a buckle (page 26, **F**). The latter joins the right strap after it passes through the transport handle of the chest-pack (page 26, below) combining the ventral and the back parachutes. On the external face of the main parachute pack frame, there is a small pocket, also found on the back of the chest-pack, containing the maintenance and folding instruction manual called 'Parachute log record'. These pockets are marked : 'Inspection and Packing data'.

When the parachute is folded, a rectangular cloth patch 'the cover' (page 31 back view refers) closes the back-pack using a cotton

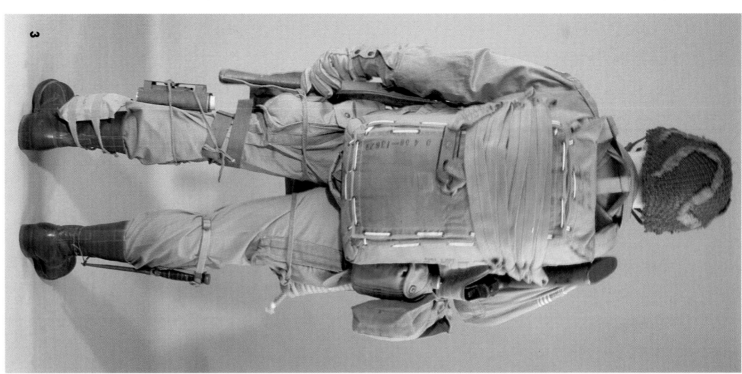
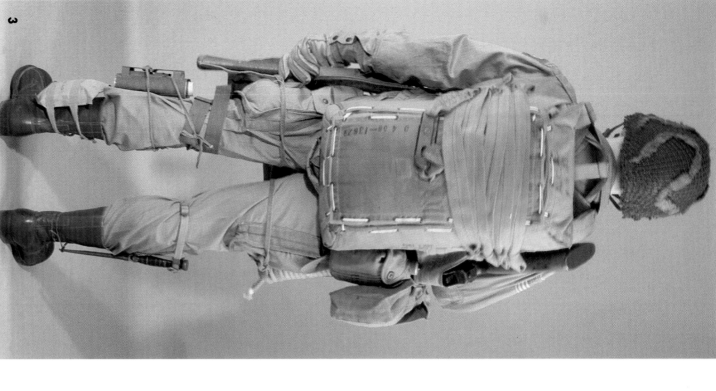

3

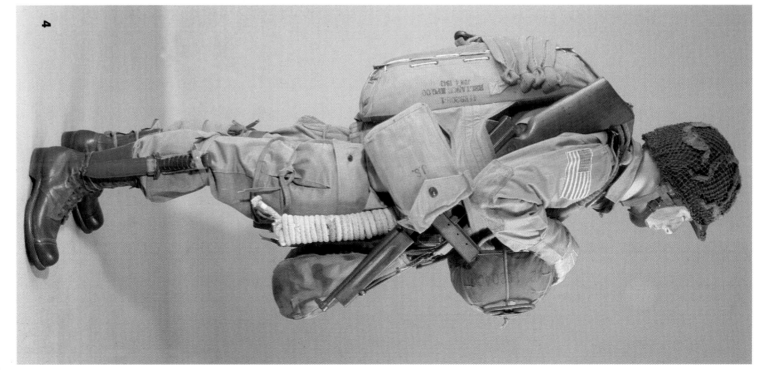

4

rope called 'breaking string'. Thanks to this rope, the cover and the pack form a homogeneous assembly.

The Static Line

It consists of a 4.60m long strap coiled on the main parachute back (page 43 back view) with elastic bands fixed on the cross-straps sewn on the pack flaps (pages 42-43 side views). One end of the static line is fixed to the cover using a very strong strap ringlet connected to the parachute through a second stap. The other end has a snap-hook attached by the paratrooper to a cable inside the aircraft (photo page 39).

When the paratrooper jumps out, the static line is pulled out, breaking the elasticated straps which secure it to the main parachute. Finally, the cover is pulled out and releases the canopy. The cover and the static line are still connected and flutter in the transport aircraft's slipstream.

The Reserve (Chest pack) Parachute

The reserve parachute's nylon or white silk canopy had a 45m² surface. Its envelope consited of a rigid rectangular frame covered by four flaps. Opening was achieved by pulling an aluminium or steel handle (often painted red).

The canopy deployed when the six elasticated straps fitted on the flaps were pulled apart, releasing the canopy.

Two snap hooks were used to secure the reserve parachute to the harness 'D' rings. The main parachute's belt strap fitted through the carrying handle of the chest pack and so, helped to secure both items together.

The Jump and the Parachutes

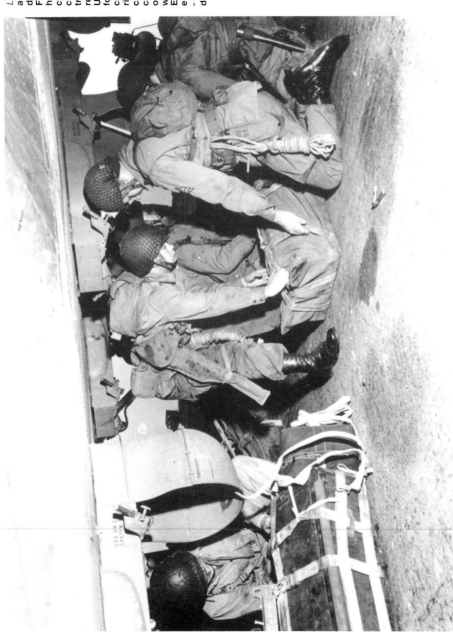

Left: Britain, early 1944. An airborne artillery squad during a training exercise. Full airborne uniform is worn: helmets with reinforced chinstrap and leather chin cup, parachute jacket and trousers plus jumpboots. The regulation issue weapon is the USM1 carbine, visible in the foreground and carried in its canvas case secured to the right side. The equipment is carried in containers or canvas 'parapacks' slung onto racks fitted under the wings of the transport aircraft. Each aircraft - with the exception of the 'leaders' - carried extra loads to the drop zone.

Right: A stick of paratroopers mustering on an Exeter base. The men belong to the 3rd Battalion, 101st A/B. Their equipment is laying on the ground in front of the aircraft. One of the two antennae of the 'Eureka-Rebecca' ground-to-air radio communication system can be seen on the aircraft nose just under the cockpit. The SCR-717 radar radome of the leader aircraft is fitted under the fuselage. The jacket of the man in the foreground, back to camera, has additional pockets made of cloth cut off from an old garment.

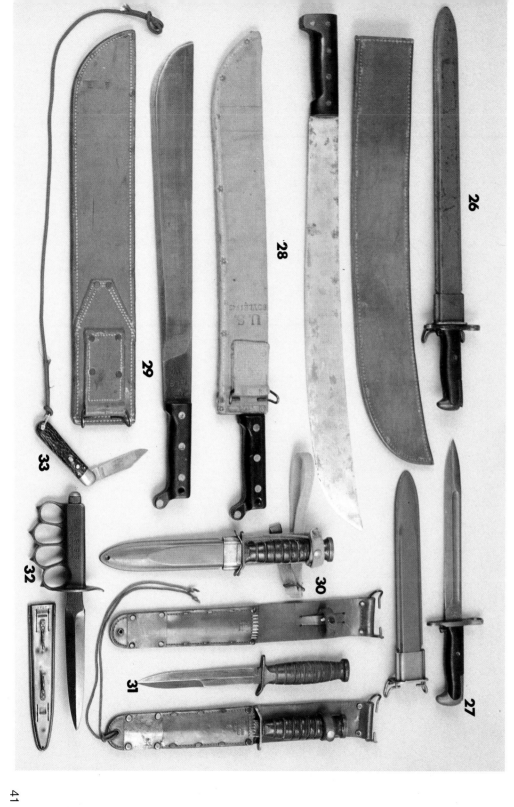

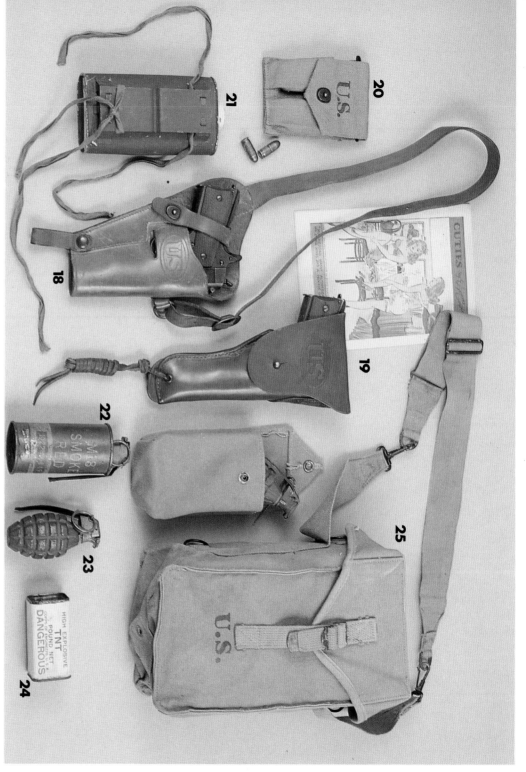

PARATROOPER EQUIPMENT

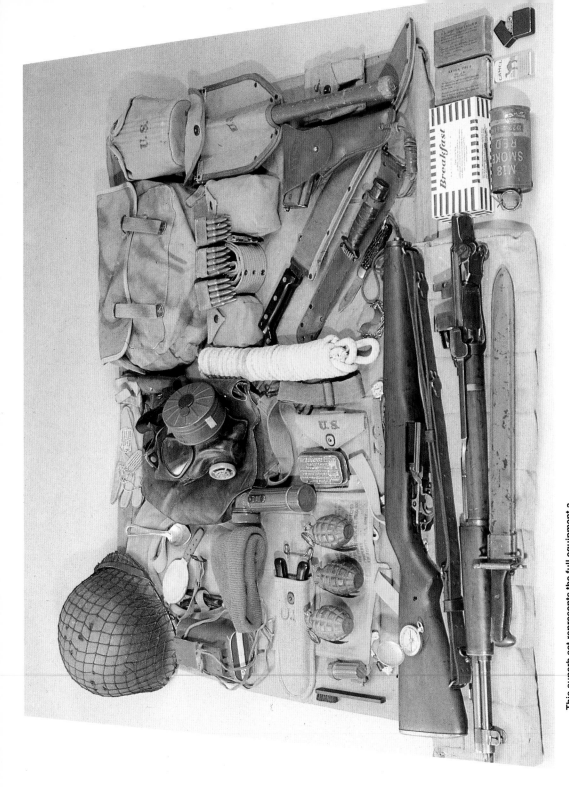

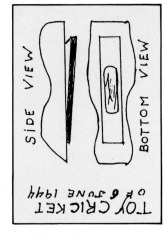

Below: Drawing made at our request in March 1987 by Tom Porcella, Veteran of the 508th P.I.R. Other veterans told us having been issued with toy crickets featuring Walt Disney's characters such as Mickey-Mouse, Donald-Duck, etc ...

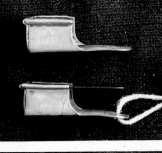

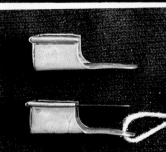

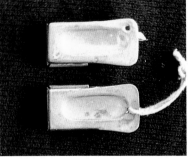

Above: Toy crickets found on the Normandy landing sites. The small hole for the cord has been punched by the paratrooper who owned the cricket. (photography thanks to the courtesy of Mr. Bazin, Avranches Museum).

This superb set represents the full equipment a paratrooper could have carried in the evening of 5 June. However, to assemble this set, the co-operation of several collectors has been necessary. Most of these items have already been described, but it is interesting to outline some others: - on the left, the model 1938 wire-cutters in their carrying case (Wirecutters M-1938) are placed on the yellow Mae-West (vest, life preserver, B4) of the USAAF; below left are a small cylindrical waterproof box of matches and a small brush to scrape the weapons.

G
enerally, the equipment issued to US Airborne troops was identical to that of regular army ground forces. However, many accessories were specifically or systematically issued to paratrooper units.

Whenever possible, all items listed in the Quartermaster Supply Catalog or the USAAF are mentioned with their official designation.

Toy Crickets

Massively distributed before D-Day, the toy cricket may not have been the most typical, butcertainly the most famous device used by US paratroopers on the night preceding the landing. Its purpose was to permit airborne troops scattered at night in enemy territory to identify friendly elements. When squeezed between thumn and forefinger, the cricket emits a 'click' amplified by the sound box. A second 'click' is produced when the pressure is released. There is no wartime regulation manual nor issue catalogue mentioning the supply of these little devices to the armed forces. Carried in a cardboard, these toy crickets only appeared in official manuals in 1945. Testimonies from 82nd and 101st Airborne veterans confirm that these toy crickets were purchased, using regimental funds, from local manufacturers or toy-retailers in Britain. □

Right: This view clearly shows the various equipment carried on operations. Note that the special chin-strap of the M1C steel helmet and its fixation straps are not visible they are folded up and hooked inside the liner, a common practice at the time.

▼ Miscellaneous Gear.

1 - Special first-aid package issued to the paratroopers (Parachute first-aid packet). The sealed waterproof canvas package contains: a garrot to stop haemorrhages, a regular bandage (package earlise model) and a small morphine syringe.

2 - M1936 Musette-bag (Bag, canvas, field, M1936). It is worn, either secured to the ringlets of the braces by two snap-hooks, or around the shoulder using an additional strap clipped to the two hooks. It is issued to all Airborne personnel regardless of their functions. The M1928 infantry haversack is however issued to the glidermen arriving from the sea as reinforcing elements. The M1936 field bag normally contains: the grooming kit, three day food supplies in K rations, the wool cap or bonnet, survival D ration, the spoon and some replacement gear. A pair of dog-tags (metal identification plates) have been placed on a M1936 bag hurriedly camouflaged with brown paint, a usual practice among invasion troops.

3 - Two K rations are placed under a survival D ration (described in 4). The breakfast and the dinner ration (the supper ration is missing). They all contain a well-balanced diet meal. The small bottle contains water purifying tablets.

4 - Survival D ration. It contains three waxed cardboard packages holding each a 113.4 gr bar of a light preparation composed of chocolate, cocoa-butter, solid skimmed-milk, sugar, oatmeal and various vitamins. The three D ration packages provide a total of 1,800 calories. This type of ration is supposed, in exceptional circumstances, to appease hunger and to restore failing energy for a period not exceeding three days.

5 - Banknotes printed in Britain or in the USA and distributed a to allied forces to purchase goods in France.

6 - Leather gloves (Gloves, horsehide, riding, unlined). The wear of leather gloves was current amongst the paratroopers. It was not a case of elegance but an essential need when coming down in brushwoods or thick bramble bushes. The typical model shown here, designed for cavalry units is common to all units.

7 - Wool cap (Skull cap). Worn under the helmet, along with the knitted cap M1941. It seems that no regulation model was in existence in the Army Ground Forces; this is probably a privately purchased item or maybe an Air Force issue to mechanics.

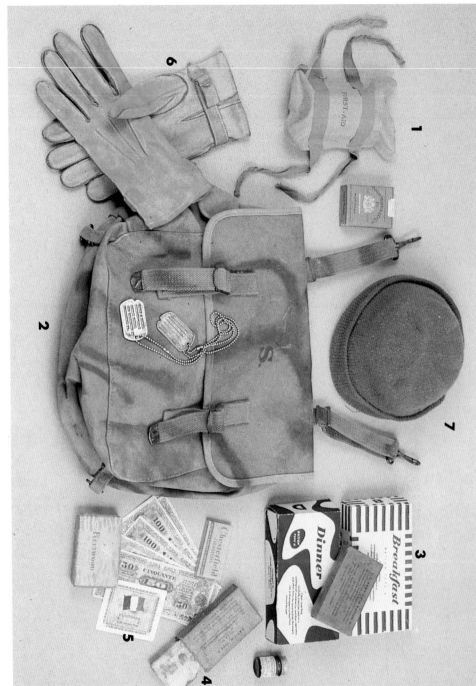

Paratrooper's Equipment

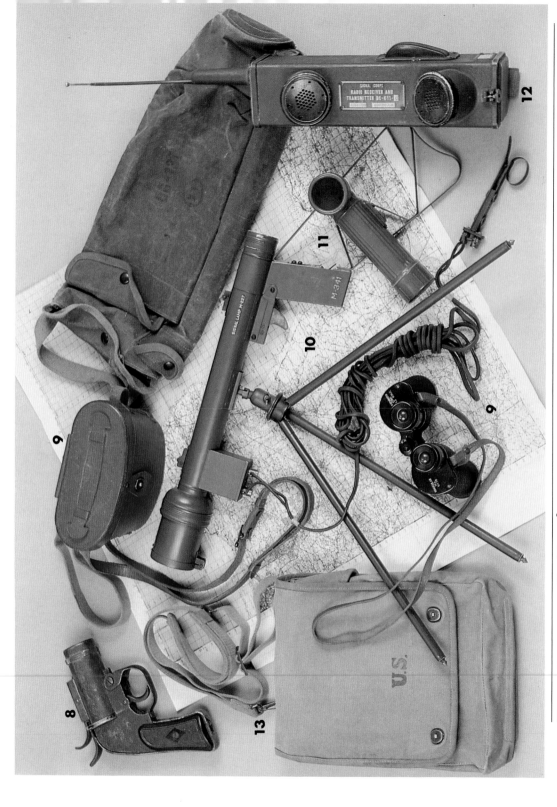

Signal and optical equipment

8 - 40 mm. cal. Flare pistol (Flare pistol AN M8). British pistols have also been distributed.

9 - Regulation infantry binoculars (Binoculars, M-3 6x30) with leather case (Case, Carrying M-17).

10 - Signal apparatus (Signal Lamp, M-227) with its canvas case. Battery operated, this transmitter transmits various coloured optical signals. It can be used as a shoulder weapon or remote controlled from a tripod. The signals are then transmitted using a telegraphic morse-type manipulator connected to the device by a cable several meters long. This set-up allows the user to operate without being exposed to ennemy fire when located.

11 - TL 122 flash light here fittted with a green lens.

12 - SCR 536 Hand-held radio receiver and transmitter (colloquially known as 'Walkie-Talkie') using a single pre-set frequency. Battery operated, it uses only vocal transmission with a collapsible antenna. It weighs 3 kg. and has a range peak-to peak of up to 1,500 m. This theoretical range is however limited due to obstacles such as: hedgerows, hills or houses.

13 - Map case (Dispatch case M1938). It contains a rhodoid cover to protect the documents; under the flap, there are several fob pockets to insert the ruler, pencils, etc. All the equipment displayed here has been placed on an ordnance map of Utah Beach showing the drop zones of the 82nd and 101st Airborne Divisions.

Gas detection and protection equipment

14 - M4 Gas mask with M10 A.1 filter. It is housed in the M6 bag containing also the cover (15), the protective goggles (16), the waterproofing kit (17) and two gas detection armbands (18).

15 - Protective cover against liquid gases (Cover, protective individual). It is removed from its sealed packing and has a transparent area for the vision.

16 - Protective goggles (Eyeshield, M.1). Copied from the British model, transparent or tinted, they are often used in dusty areas.

17 - Gas mask waterproofing kit for amphibious operations (Kit, gas mask, waterproofing, M.I).

18 - Gas detection armband (Sleeve gas detector). This armband is manufactured in a kind of heavy light brown paper, impregnated with a chemical product which in contact with noxious gas, turns to blue or pink according to the nature of the gas. A reinforcing cloth strap around it has a buckle to insert the right shoulder strap. This armband is not specific to airborne units. It is of regular issue to all the troops involved in the landing operations, each fighter receiving two.

19 - Waterproof gas mask and bag specially designed for amphibious operations (Amphibious Assault Gas Mask M-5, Filter M-11, Bag M-7). On june 6, 1944, the whole of the assault formations coming either from the sea or the air, were issued with this type of gas mask which was withdrawn and replaced by the standard model (14) in the following days.

Ground survie and escape equipment

20 - Cardboard package containing an escape and orientation kit : map of Normandy printed on cloth, miniature metal saw, French money, tiny compass (refer to the 'Parachute' chapter). For obvious security reasons, this package was only delivered when the full elements of the two Airborne divisions were assembled on their take-off zones. Unless in possession of a special pass, nobody was allowed 'in' or 'out'.

21 - Issue compass with its canvas case (US Army Corps of Engineers Compass). Usually reserved for officers or men assigned to a special orientation mission.

22 - Plactic wrist compasses with original leather strap and canvas strap. The general issue isnot so sophisticad.

23 - Regulation compass of the 'fob-watch' type.

24 - Metal and plastic whistles used by the NCO's for assembling or commanding the troops. They are carried in the left breast pocket, their thin chain fixed to the shoulder strap.

25 - Issue wrist watch.

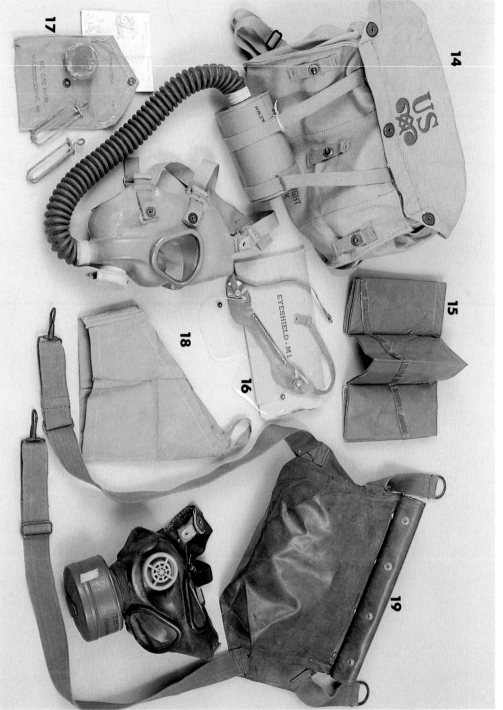

AIRBORNE UNIT'S INSIGNIA

Among the various insignias currently seen on Airborne troops uniforms, one can clearly distinguish those used on combat dress for identification purposes and those used to 'embellish' the service and walking-out dress.

Above: Three types of national flag insignia. Worn on the right sleeve. See text for details.

Left: National flag insignia, small type, identical to N° 1. Sewn on a jacket found in the Pont-l'Abbé area, the white edges have the regulation width.

There are two kind of insignias worn in combat. On D-Day, apart for their rank insignia, the paratroopers and the glidermen only wore their unit patch (on the shoulder) and the national flag, typical for offensive operations involving landing or parachute drops in enemy or occupied territory.

The National Identification Flag

Concerned about possible brutal reactions from the ennemy in case of capture[1] and in order to allow French civilians to identify and help the invaders, Allied High Command distributed just before D-Day, small American flags to be sewn at the top of the right arm (this was already used in North Africa during Operation Torch in 1942). Although wartime documents show that these were not distributed to each man, we can distinguish three main types (see top photograph).

1. Small coarse-cloth model (12 x 7 cm). The worn are thinner than originally.

2. Small plastified canvas type (13 x 7 cm). Note the machine-stitching.

3. Large type in plastified canvas (13 x 9.5 cm) cut-out in the canvas armband held by two safety-pins. Judged inefficient, this armband was probably always used cut and sewn.

Various Badges and Insignia

There are three main categories of badges worn by Airborne and Glider units: the unit insignias, the qualification badges and the hat badges, not always worn in combat.

The unit insignia

The main unit insignia encompass the divisional patches worn at the top of the left sleeve by the 82nd and the 101st Airborne, but also the general USAAF insignia or the 9th Air For-

1. According to an order given by Hitler himself, (N°. 003830/42-GKDOS. CKW. West of 10/18/1942) it was prescribed that German forces summarily execute the Allied soldiers participating in commando operations, even in uniform with the exception of those captured during a large-scale operation. During the night of 6 June, the Germans of course had no possibility to determine any of those cases!

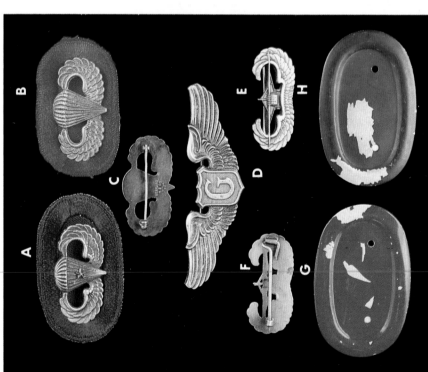

QUALIFICATION BADGES, INSIGNIA AND WINGS OVALS

A - A rare parachute qualification badge with a (unofficial) superimposed star indicating the participation to a combat jump. The oval is that of infantry. The qualification badge is received after five training jumps or one operational jump without training.

B - Standard badge on red artillery patch.

C - Back view of a badge made in the USA. This particular badge was worn on June 5, 1944 by Robert M. Murphy, Pathfinder of the 505th P.I.R.

D - Glider pilot badge issued in September 1942 (US–AF).

E - Glider badge (all branches) received after a combat operation. Officially approved in March 1944.

F - Back view of a badge made in Britain. Compare the pin with that of 'C'.

G - Locally made stamped wings (Artillery).

H - Same model for Infantry.

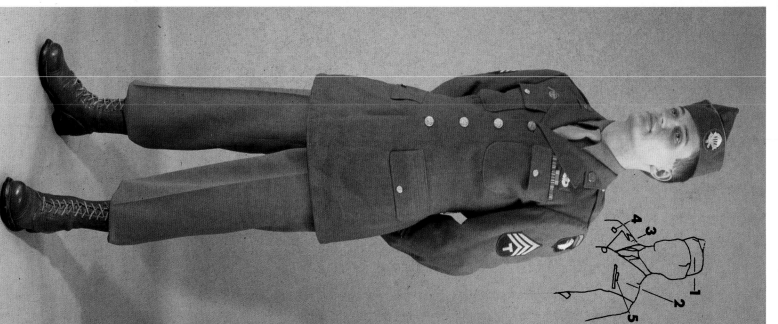

Above: 1946. The war is over. Back in the USA, this 4th Grade Technician of the 326th Engineer Battalion, 101st Airborne has slipped on his walking-out uniform for the last time before returning definitively to civilian clothes.
Description of the winter uniform:
1 - Garrison cap piped in red and white, branch colour of the Corps of Engineers. As for all enlisted-men and NCO's wearing their ranks on the sleeve, the standard Airborne round patch is sewn on the left side.
2 - Serge-type wool jacket for enlisted personnel, of the model adopted in 1942 (Coat Wool, Serge).
3 - Collar disks : on the right, the US monogram, on the left the mini castle representing the Corps of Engineers.
4 - Honourable discharge emblem (familiarly called *'Ruptured Duck'* awarded on discharge by all army personnel having served with honour and devotion.
5 - Embroidered parachute qualification wings on green background. This particular set-up makes believe that the 'beloved' sterling silver original badge has been left as a souvenir in the handbag of a pretty Parisian girl!

Back in Britain after the campaign, this young Captain of the 505th Parachute Infantry Regiment has slipped on his smartest uniform (Class 'A' dress) to pose for the 'souvenir-picture' in a London studio. This officer wears the wool service coat with the famous pink trousers of the same material which was a big surprise to other Allied troops. He also wears the non-regulation pink garrison cap with black and gold piping for officers. Although supposed to set an example, he has kept his jump boots, practice strictly forbidden by regulations, but which distinguished paratroopers from regular troopers. Insignias and awards are worn as perm regulations:
1 - Captain Silver rank bars.
2 - Standard Airborne round patch sewn on the right as prescribed for officers.
3 - Regular officers insignias on the lapels, the US monograms above the Infantry crossed rifles.
4 - The blue bar of the 'Presidential Unit Citation', distinction awarded to a full unit for exemplary behaviour on the battlefield (the 505th P.I.R. was awarded this distinction for its action in Ste-Mère-

Eglise from 6 to 9 June, 1944).
5 - Parachute qualification badge.
6 - Combat Infantryman badge (light-blue rectangle with musket rifle surrounded by palms). Instituted on November 15, 1943, it is only awarded to officers and men having proved their valour and competence on the front line. Its attribution, restricted to infantry units, comprises a 10 $ premium. Among the plethora of insignias, badges and medals worn by the soldiers, this badge is one of a few of a certain 'value' as allowing to spot the real fighters from the 'shirkers'. This officer does not comply with regulations as this badge cannot be worn along with the parachute qualification badge.
7 - Medal ribbons
8 - Overseas service stripes embroidered in yellow thread or in gold bullion; each bar indicates six months of overseas service. Below, the bronzed-colored stripe sewn around the sleeves on the officer's coats and overcoats.

Left: Probably not a 'needlework' expert, this paratrooper of the 82nd Airborne has just fixed his shoulder sleeve insignia with large stitches. The man's name has been stencilled in black above the left pocket. A current practice among Airborne forces. This was sometimes seen in other units by using a small printed cloth band sewn on the uniform. This private comforting a wounded prisoner wears a reinforced uniform and one can notice the pencils stuck in the fob pocket behind the flap of the breast pocket are noteworthy. He is also wearing the issue woollen gloves with leather palm.

Above: This 'Screaming Eagle' of the 101st A/B has been captured. Facing the photographer, his smiling is significant, realising that soon, the roles will be reversed. One can clearly see the shoulder sleeve insignia sewn exactly at the regulation place using large white thread stitches; there is no place for aesthetic considerations on combat uniforms.

Right: Possibly in direct lineage of Mohican indians (there are some authentic ones in the US Army), the privates C.C. Ware and C.R. Plaudo are finishing their ritual make-up, typical of those 'wild' and proud tribes. They both wear an indian style haircut and one can imagine the reaction of the german soldiers (as well as the french civilians!) seeing those guys surging from the night with such a look. The completely shaved heads currently seen among the US paratroopers are not the result of a military fashion, but a recommendation of the Medical Corps: in case of injury at the skull, the hair might be a source of infection or complication for the medics in charge of cleaning the wound. The face cammouflage, often made using soot or partially burned corks, can also be done – and it is the case here with a special black, green or beige paste made by cosmetic manufacturers, issued in tubes by the Quartermaster. The man on the right also judged indispensable the current practice of adding an extra pocket on the sleeve of his jacket and to maintain the 'Esprit de Corps' always present, the famous 'Screaming Eagle' of the 101st A/B has been sewn on the flap. Favourite models of the US paratroopers, the clear-skin gloves 'Horseman style' are clearly visible here as well as the high capacity ammunition pouches. Notice near the SMG Thompson magazine, the CS-34 leather case containing the small tools used to install telephone lines: pliers and folding-knife with screwdriver-blade.

Airborne Units' Insignia

ce patch of the glider pilots. These shoulder patches are worn on both the combat and walking-out uniforms. Some non-regulation pocket patches were also sewn on the pockets of the shirt or jacket in some P.I.R. These patches were normally not worn in combat.

Only worn on the service coat, the distinctive insignias are small enamelled heraldic badges representing a regiment or a battalion. They were pinned on to the officer's shoulder straps and on the lower lapels of enlisted-mens jackets. Considering the number of fighting units, it looks like most of them never had or had worn such an insignia. One must also note that even the models shown in our displays, were rarely distributed, due to the restrictions enforced by the State Department, covering certain strategic metals such as copper and bronze.

In fact, unit insignias were used as collar badges by the officers. They represented the branch of service often coupled to the battalion number. They are pinned on the left collar on the combat and service dress. A larger badge is available for the coat.

Qualification Badges

There are three types of qualification badges : the parachute qualification badge, the glider and the glider pilot badge. They were worn above the left breast pocket of the service uniform. Our display shows 'wings' in spe-

cific to Airborne troops on which the qualification badges described above are pinned or embroidered. The oval background usually indicates the branch color and, being 'unofficial' only approved after the war. Most of the time, these were made of felt, cut cloth or more rarely painted on metal. Except for the 501st P.I.R., all the ovals shown have been made in the 1950s; the form and color are however exactly the same as original insignia.

Cap Insignia

These were sewn on the garrison cap (overseas cap) worn by Airborne troops. The origin of those garrison cap airborne patches are, specific to those units and dated back to 1941. At the time, the officers of the 501st Battalion really wanted to distinguish their men from regular infantry. Therefore, they had round light-blue cloth insignia manufactured bordered in white and bearing a white parachute (light-blue being the branch color for infantry as shown on the piping of the garrison cap). During the summer of 1942, this initiative was extended to all existing Airborne troops, Artillery and Engineer units wearing a patch with red background. These models were never officially approved.

Up to 25 April, 1942, all units wore the insignia on the left side of the cap, but from that date on, order was given to officers to wear their rank badge at this place; therefore, the

AIRBORNE TROOPS' INSIGNIA

Insignia	Uniform and location
SHOULDER SLEEVE INSIGNIA	At the top of the left sleeve, 1.27 cm from the shoulder seam. Officers : summer and winter service coats shirt (worn alone), overcoat, sometimes raincoat, combat uniform.
QUALIFICATION BADGES	On the left breast, service coat, shirt a (worn alone), exceptionally on combat uniform
DISTINCTIVE INSIGNIA (pocket patches)	Officers: on the shoulder straps of the service coat. NCO's and men: on the lower lapels of the service coat. On the left breast pocket of sport or training outfits. For the officers, exceptionally on the combat uniform (for example USAAF leather jacket bought at the p. X.). Sometimes seen on enlisted-mens shirt pockets
CAP INSIGNIA	On the brown or beige garrison cap, on the right for officers, on the left for NCO's and men.
NATIONAL IDENTIFICATION FLAG	At the top of the right arm for all personnel. On combat uniform only.

round patch will be switched to the right side. However, some 'hard cases' went to the point of wearing their rank badge pinned on the round cloth insignia remaining on the left. During that summer, a similar type of insignia was issued for gliders troups, showing a white embroidered glider, facing right for the officers and left for NCO's and men. Finally, in the spring of 1943, a unique insignia was issued by the Airborne Command to solve the problem of numerous variations. These variations

were uses anyway in spite of numerous official directives.

For almost every insignia, described above, one can find the existence of fancy variations, most of the time locally made at the initiative of the Commanding officer when no official manufacture existed: they were purchased at the P.X., especially the embroidered insignia or high quality badges for the walking-out uniform. □

Above: **Some time before the 'longest Day', these three paratroopers stroll in a green square around Nottingham. From left to right, the privates Downes, Cleaver and Levesque are resplandent in their service dress. Normally forbidden with this uniform, the jump boots are polished like mirrors. Notice on the left side of the chest, the typical oval insignia of airborne troops. According to US Army summertime regulations, the man in the centre wears, the woollen shirt with the tie inserted between the 2nd and 3rd button (Photo Tom Porcella).**

INSIGNIA OF THE 82nd AIRBORNE DIVISION

1 - Shoulder sleeve insignia approved in October 1918. The addition of an Airborne tab occured in August 1942, when it was converted from an Infantry division to an Airborne unit. The two back-meaning that this unit is composed of men from all the American states.

2 - Non regulation model embroidered in bullion for officers and veterans. Postwar german made.

3 - Cloth oval patch - 505th Parachute Infantry Regiment.

4 - Cloth oval patch - 307th Engineer Battalion.

5 - Cloth oval patch - 325th Glider Infantry Regiment with gliderborne troops badge.

6 - Stamped metal variation with painting of the 325th P.I.R. (locally made).

7 - Cloth oval - 508th P.I.R. with embroidered parachute qualification wings.

8 - Pocket patch, early model of the 508th P.I.R. (unofficial).

9 - Officer's service coat lapel branch insignia.

10 - Pocket patch, 2nd model of the 508th P.I.R. 'The Red Devils' (unofficial).

DISTINCTIVE METAL INSIGNIA

11.12 - Metal divisional insignia, (small and middle size). These were worn by members of the units whitout specific insignia (non-regulation models sold at the P.X.).

13 - 80th A.B. Anti-Aircraft Artillery Battalion.

14 - 307th A.B. Engineer Battalion Glider.

15 - 319th Field Artillery Battalion Glider.

16 - 320th Field Artillery Battalion Glider.

17 - Officers' service coat lapel branch insignia of the 320th Field Artillery Battalion.

18 - 376th Field Artillery Parachute Battalion.

INSIGNIA OF THE 101st AIRBORNE DIVISION

19 - Divisional insignia of the 'Screaming Eagles'. Officially approved on May 29, 1923. Converted to Airborne division on August 28, 1942 (European manufacture shown here on black velvet background).

20 - Non regulation model embroidered in bullion for officers and veterans. Postwar German made model.

21 - Pocket patch, 501st Parachute Infantry Regiment (unofficial).

22 - Cloth oval, 501st P.I.R. (original patch).

23 - Cloth oval, 506th Parachute Infantry Regiment.

24 - Cloth oval, 326th A/B Engineer battalion.

25 - Pocket patch, 506th.

P.I.R. METAL DISTINCTIVE INSIGNIA

26 - Metal divisional insignia, small size. Same use and origin as 11 and 12.

27 - 501st Parachute Infantry Regiment.

28 - 502nd P.I.R.

29 - 506th P.I.R. As a reminder, the insignia shown here was issued in the 1950s. From the six Paratrooper Infantry Regiments at the time, the 506th is the only one not to be issued with a metal distinctive insignia

30 - 327th Infantry Regiment Glider.

31 - 321st Field Artillery Battalion Glider.

32 - 377th F.A.B. Parachute.

33 - 463rd F.A.B. Parachute.

34 - Officers' service coat lapel branch insignia of the 321st Field Artillery Battalion.

35 - 907th Field Artillery Battalion Glider.

The insignias of the airborne units

CAP INSIGNIA

36 - Officer pink garrison cap. General airborne insignia issued in 1943 (officially replaces all the variations described hereafter).

37 - Officer garrison cap (winter uniform).Early model insignia.

38 - NCO's and other ranks' garrison cap (light-blue piping for Infantry).

39 - Same model in cotton (summer uniform).

40 - Garrison cap with insignia of Gliderborne Infantry.

41 - Garrison cap of the Corps of Engineers (piped in white and red) with general airborne insignia issued to Airborne units in 1943.

42 - NCO's and other ranks' garrison cap of the USAAF (piped in blue and orange) with the distinctive insignia of the Troop Carrier Command.

43 - Airborne Infantry. Early model, French made, silver bullion embroidery (non regulation, should not be worn at the time).

44 - Artillery and Parachute Engineers. 45. Airborne Infantry and Gliders (NCO's and other ranks').

46 - Gliders (all branches).

47 - Gliders (officers').

48 - Gliders, (artillery).

49 - Cloth reduced-sized model, similar to 11 and 12 (may be worn on civilian clothes).

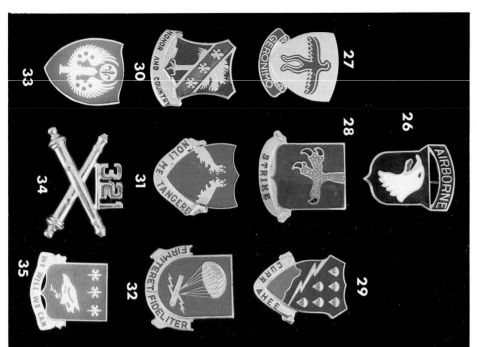

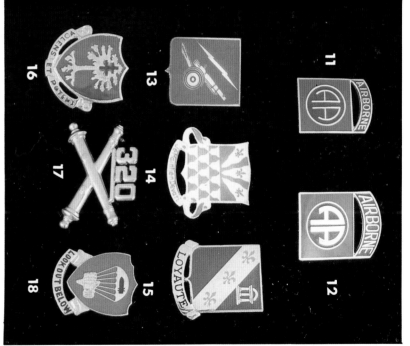

Basic Table of organisation of the American Airborne Divisions on 6 June 1944

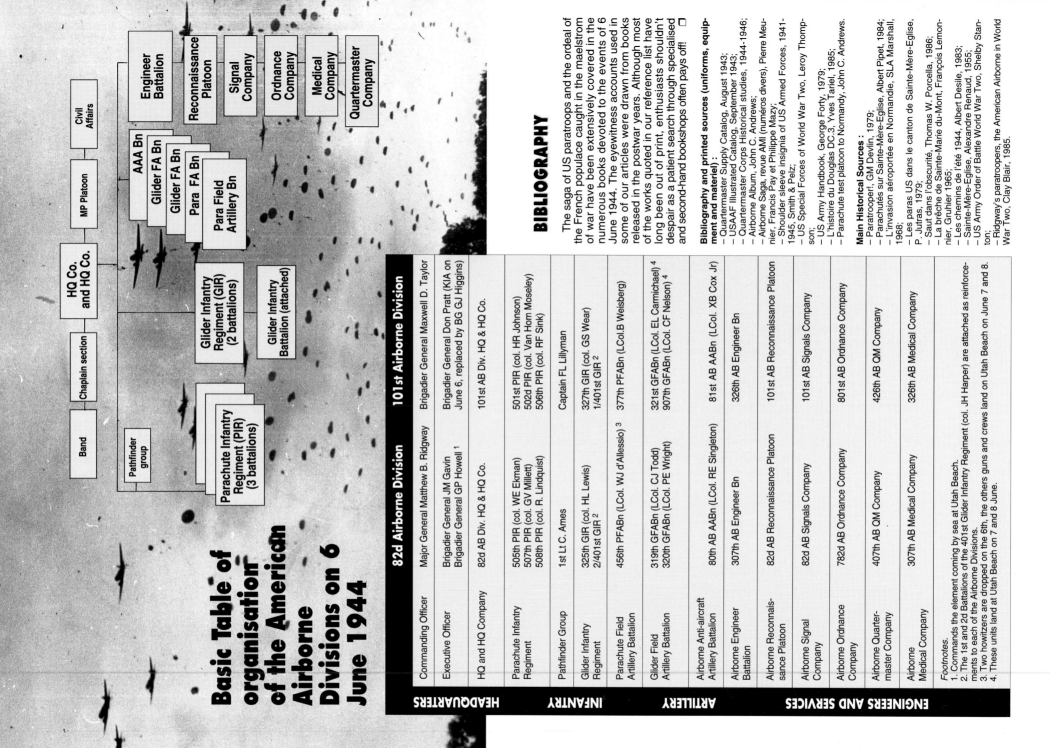

		82d Airborne Division	101st Airborne Division
HEADQUARTERS	Commanding Officer	Major General Matthew B. Ridgway	Brigadier General Maxwell D. Taylor
	Executive Officer	Brigadier General JM Gavin / Brigadier General GP Howell [1]	Brigadier General Don Pratt (KIA on June 6, replaced by BG GJ Higgins)
	HQ and HQ Company	82d AB Div. HQ & HQ Co.	101st AB Div. HQ & HQ Co.
INFANTRY	Parachute Infantry Regiment	505th PIR (col. WE Ekman) / 507th PIR (col. GV Millett) / 508th PIR (col. R. Lindquist)	501st PIR (col. HR Johnson) / 502d PIR (col. Van Horn Moseley) / 506th PIR (col. RF Sink)
	Pathfinder Group	1st Lt C. Ames	Captain FL Lillyman
	Glider Infantry Regiment	325th GIR (col. HL Lewis) 2/401st GIR [2]	327th GIR (col. GS Wear) 1/401st GIR [2]
ARTILLERY	Parachute Field Artillery Battalion	456th PFABn (LCol. WJ d'Allessio) [3]	377th PFABn (LCol.B Weisberg)
	Glider Field Artillery Battalion	319th GFABn (LCol. CJ Todd) / 320th GFABn (LCol. PE Wright)	321st GFABn (LCol. EL Carmichael) [4] / 907th GFABn (LCol. CF Nelson) [4]
	Airborne Anti-aircraft Artillery Battalion	80th AB AABn (LCol. RE Singleton)	81st AB AABn (LCol. XB Cox Jr)
ENGINEERS AND SERVICES	Airborne Engineer Battalion	307th AB Engineer Bn	326th AB Engineer Bn
	Airborne Reconnaissance Platoon	82d AB Reconnaissance Platoon	101st AB Reconnaissance Platoon
	Airborne Signal Company	82d AB Signals Company	101st AB Signals Company
	Airborne Ordnance Company	782d AB Ordnance Company	801st AB Ordnance Company
	Airborne Quartermaster Company	407th AB QM Company	426th AB QM Company
	Airborne Medical Company	307th AB Medical Company	326th AB Medical Company

Footnotes.
1. Commands the element coming by sea at Utah Beach.
2. The 1st and 2d Battalions of the 401st Glider Infantry Regiment (col. JH Harper) are attached as reinforcements to each of the Airborne Divisions.
3. Two howitzers are dropped on the 6th, the others guns and crews land on Utah Beach on June 7 and 8.
4. These units land at Utah Beach on 7 and 8 June.

BIBLIOGRAPHY

The saga of US paratroops and the ordeal of the French populace caught in the maelstrom of war have been extensively covered in the numerous books devoted to the events of 6 June 1944. The eyewitness accounts used in some of our articles were drawn from books released in the postwar years. Although most of the works quoted in our reference list have long been out of print, enthusiasts shouldn't despair as a patient search through specialised and second-hand bookshops often pays off!

Bibliography and printed sources (uniforms, equipment and materiel) :
– Quartermaster Supply Catalog, August 1943;
– USAAF Illustrated Catalog, September 1943;
– Quartermaster Corps Historical studies, 1944-1946;
– Airborne Album, John C. Andrews;
– Airborne Saga, revue AMI (numéros divers), Pierre Meunier, Francis Pay et Philippe Mazy;
– Shoulder sleeve insignia of US Armed Forces, 1941-1945, Smith & Pelz;
– US Special Forces of World War Two, Leroy Thompson;
– US Army Handbook, George Forty, 1979;
– L'histoire du Douglas DC.3, Yves Tariel, 1985;
– Parachute test platoon to Normandy, John C. Andrews.

Main Historical Sources :
– Paratrooper!, GM Devlin, 1979;
– Parachutés sur Sainte-Mère-Eglise, Albert Pipet, 1984;
– L'invasion aéroportée en Normandie, SLA Marshall, 1968;
– Les paras US dans le canton de Sainte-Mère-Eglise, P. Jutras, 1979;
– Saut dans l'obscurité, Thomas W. Porcella, 1986;
– La brèche de Sainte-Marie du-Mont, François Lemonnier, Gruhier 1965;
– Les chemins de l'été 1944, Albert Desile, 1983;
– Sainte-Mère-Eglise, Alexandre Renaud, 1955;
– US Army Order of Battle World War Two, Shelby Stanton;
– Ridgway's paratroopers, the American Airborne in World War Two, Clay Blair, 1985.

It is impossible to assess precisely the number of men from the 82nd and 101st Airborne divisions who became casualties during the Normandy operations; it is clear that in the heat of the battle - and considering the large number of missing soldiers - the commanding officers had other things in mind than counting their men! As the 82nd A/B participated and was not relieved until July 8; and that the 101st A/B had to face, after the capture of Carentan, the counter-attack of the 17th SS, and the 6th Fallschirmjäger Regt., the total casualties at the end of the campaign (wounded, killed and missing in action) are estimated by the most reliable sources as follows:

- 'Paratroopers!' par G.M. Develin (1979): 82nd: 5,245. 101st : 4,670.
- 'Parachutés sur Ste Mère Eglise' (1947): 82nd: 4,480, 101st: 4670.
- 'Utah Beach to Cherbourg'. Historical Department U.S Army A.Piper (1984) 82nd: 4,355, 101st: 3,936.

Some of those figures are very close to each other and even identical in one case. Some important discrepancies remain, maybe due to the probably different dates not mentioned in the survey. The 'missing in action' denomination may be confusing as it includes the prisoners, the elements lost during the jump and who joined their unit later, and the unlucky ones swallowed up for ever in the murky waters of the marshes of the Douve and the Merderet.

Below: In a Cotentin farmyard, the General Omar N. Bradley, Commanding the first Army is decorating some officers and men of the 82nd Airborne division. The soldier leaning on a stick is Lieutenant-Colonel B.H. Vandervoort, commanding the 2nd Battalion of the 505th P.I.R. His name is stencilled above his upper left pocket; his rank badges are pinned as on a shirt, the silver oak leaves are on the collar lapels. The Medic in the center, unarmed as per the Geneva convention, is wearing a standard MI helmet with the first type of liner (rounded thicker rim). Noticeable by their laced boots, the two paratroopers on the right have discarded their badly worn jump suits and wear instead woollen shirt and trousers. The neat pleats of the garments show that they are fresh from storage. The three officers on the left wear trousers with straps to hold the pockets. Their rank insignias are shown on the front of the helmet. The Captain on the left of Vandervoort has hooked a quickly-made pouch on his cartridge-belt which could hold two grenades.

Excerpts from a wartime manual, the drawings represent three possibilities of building visual signals with several panels:

1 ..... We attack.

2 ..... Ammunition needed.

3 ..... The ennemy attacks.

To visually communicate with the Air Force, the paratroopers dispose signal panels (Panel AL 141). They consisted of plastified canvas rectangular panels measuring 3.66 m x 0.82 m. One face was bright orange and the other plain white. Straps around them allowed to secure them to the ground or attach them to a vehicle. Each panel was carried in a webbing case (Case CS 150) closed by a fixing lug located at one edge and fitted with a strap allowing to carry it on the shoulder or slung.

USAAF AND AIRBORNE FORCES INSIGNIA

58 - Shoulder sleeve insignia of the Airborne Command. Created in March 1942, this Command was in charge of training and putting into action all Airborne units. Its designation changed on March 1, 1944 to 'The Airborne Center'. The patch, approved in March 1943 exists with a separate Airborne tab.

59 - 2nd Airborne Infantry Brigade. Temporary unit created in Britain in January 1944, including the 501st and 508th P.I.R. These two units were respectively incorporated later on to the 101st and 82nd Airborne.

60 - Pocket patch worn on sport outfit or civilian clothes. Unofficial and never sewn on any uniform.

61 - US Army Air Force general insignia. It is worn on D-Day by the glider pilots simultaneously with patch 62.

62 - 9th Air Force patch, unit of all the glider pilots (the Colonel Emil Mares, USAAF veteran of the D-Day ,ex-glider pilot confirmed to us in a letter of March 1987 that he as worn this shoulder patch.

63 - Insignia of the 1st Troop Carrier Command, in charge of the training of glider pilots.

64 - Non-regulation insignia worn by the crews of the USAAF aircraft tasked with dropping men and equipment as well as towing the gliders.

65 - Distinctive insignia of the 401st Infantry Glider Regiment.

66 - Small metal variation of the No. 63 worn on the garrison cap.

Below: Unlike their British counterparts of the Glider Pilot Regiment answering to army ground forces and engaged in the combats after the landing, these US glider pilots are connected to the US Army Air Force and wore the insignia of this service: USAAF general insignia on top of the left arm and USAAF officer badge on the shirt's collar. Although fully equipped as regular infantrymen in case evacuation was impossible, they are commenting on their extraordinary adventure situation to be removed from the front line. Repatriated to England, these glider pilots are commenting on their extraordinary adventure but their grins show that everything did not go like clockwork. Note on the man next to him is leaning on a G. 98K Mauser rifle brought back as a souvenir; this weapon might be today decorating the the fire place of a ranch in Texas or Arkansas.

GO TO IT!

5 June, in the evening. The dynamic motto of the 6th Airborne, devised by Major General Gale himself while taking over command, will now earn its proper meaning.

At 22 h 56, at the RAF Tarrant Rushton airfield, six Horsa type gliders under the command of major Howard are taking off, towed by their large Halifax quad engines. Seven minutes later, at Harwell base, 60 Pathfinders belonging to the 22nd Independant Company of the army air corps are emptying their tea mugs, stub out their cigarettes, and haul themselves to the cabins of the six Albemarle twin-engined planes. They will form the spearhead of the immense armada constituted by the 38th and 46th Groups of the RAF Transport Command wich carries the main body of the 6th division. All base personnel not on duty is massed along the runways, shouting to show their support to the airborne troops, by now crowded together in their planes and gliders, trying to suppress their emotion, while at a short distance, a sizeable number of Waaf and Naafi personnel stealthily wipe away an occasional tear. Suddenly, a flash lights up from the control tower. The pilot realease the brakes, accelerate their engines to full throttle and leave the runways in rapid succession. The dice is cast!

The 6th Airborne Division

In May 1943, the 6th Airborne is officially formed in britain, and during the subsequent months, the various corps composing the division are assembled and based in barracks at the plains of Salisbury (Wiltshire). Incorporated into the field army, the British Airborne Division in 1944 is similarly composed along the lines wich essentialy make up a standard infantry division consisting of three brigades with three batallions each. We remark, however, the fact that the infantry division's support units areb are substituted by an Army Air Corps Pathfinder Group.

Two brigades will be purely parachutists (para brigades), the third being glider infantry (airlanding brigade). Each of these comprise engineer and medical units, among others. Support and maintenance units, however will be considerably reduced. On 6 June, the available transport only permit the airlift of ca 7500 men,

Above: On 4 June, Major General Gale gathered his men for a final briefing. Addressing them in small groups, he gave details about the Allies' plans. The group of soldiers depicted above includes men from the Parachute Regiment and airborne soldiers of the 6th Airlanding Brigade. In the left foreground, the Ox and Bucks titles are clearly visible as well as the 'Glider' qualification badges sewn on a 'Light Infantry' green background. The sitting officer displays the white parachute sleeve insignia awarded to personnel unassigned to an active airborne unit. All the officers in the picture wear the tie/open collar arrangement. (IWM).

Left: 4 June, somewhere in Britain, airborne troopers scrutinizing their advance pay, conciciting of newly issued invasion-money bills adorned with the French tricolore. The two men seen at right belong the Royal Corps of Signal of wich they are wearing the cap badge pinned on a maroon beret. Under their brown flannel shirt, the string vest is clearly visible (see the signalman at right). We clearly remark the identification number on the shirt of the soldier at left, whose sleeve is also adorned with airborne wings, a non-regulation practice, but nevertheless occuring.

amounting to two thirds of the division (total effective more than 12 000 men). Starting on 7 June, the remaining part will be transported by ships.

The Red Berets, Herculean Tasks

4 June, troops of the 6th Airborne are assembled in tents camps unaccessible to anyone not carrying a special pass. By now, all are aware of their mission. All over the camp, Major-General Gale is observed instilling the importance of their tasks to the men. Being a straightforward commander he does not conceal the perils lying ahead 'The Huns consider it sheer folly to engage them at the designated area, wich is my main reason to undertake the challenge!', he declares while outlining the Orne river on the map. Meanwhile, he is being watched by attentive and earnest faces, since this job will be an entirely different matter compared to

the occasional fist-fights with the yanks from the 101st Airborne conducted at the local pubs. The task of the 6th British Airborne Division, reinforced by the 1st Special Service Brigade is as follows: to protect the left flank of the 1st Corps by occupying the sector between the Orne and la Dives rivers. By deploying on the Troan-Sanneville-Colombelless line, every attack coming from Caen should be repelled.

The missions of the threerd Para Brigade:
- to capture the artillery battery at Merville and destroy its cannon.
- to destroy the Dives and Divette river bridge situated Troam-Bures-Robehomme-Varaville.
- lock up the roads between Troam-Sannerville-Troarn-Escoville, Robehomme-Le Mesnil, Merri-Breville, and the Franceville-Sallenelles beach.

Ranville, 6 June, 1944 2.30 am

This modest farmer town will be enter history as the first-French town to be liberated'. far from being an insignificant hamlet, it was a typical small French community inhabited by 560 people, having its own town hall, post-office, school, church, blacksmith and cartwright shop. Town life was further enlightened by its five cafés equiped to serve hearty meals.

After a brief struggle, Ranville was solidly held by the para's of the 13th Batallion (Lancashire) of the parachute regiment. simultaneously, the first flag to fell in Allied hands on D-Day was captured, a feat accomplished by Major R.M. Tarrant, an officer belonging to the Dorsetshire Regiment, engaged in combat along with the 5th Para Brigade. Severly wounded on 19 August, at Putot en Auge, he would die on 28 August, at the Douvres la Delivrande military hospital.

1. Strictly historically speaking, Corsica was the first french department to be liberated.

The 5th Brigade's missions are:
- the seizure of the bridges crossing the Orne and the Ranville and Bénouville canals.
- to grab the Bénouville-Ranville-Bas sector
- to relieve and occupy the zone east of Ranville

Go to it!

Above: **Standing in front of a Stirling, a RAF sergeant assists a paratrooper buckling his X-type parachute. In the leg bag behind the sergeant's back we observe the handle of an infantrey field shovel, as well as the barrel and muzzle of a Sten Mark V machine carbine. The man at left is wearing his toggle rope like a belt on wich is attached his spike bayonet. None of them wear the oversmock, cetainly to avoid hampering while landing.**

Above: Night has fallen on RAF Hartwell air base. Major-General Gale is seen boarding the aircraft which will take him to Normandy. Wearing a maroon beret adorned with his rank badge, the officer has donned a Denison smock and beige woollen riding breeches. His combat boots have been polished to a high gloss by his batman. A stick completes the uniform. Behind the general, on the right, stands a staff officer wearing a Mk II helmet and a modified Denison smock. He has stuffed his maroon beret into his right pocket. Carried in the right pocket, the officer's handgun is secured by a lanyard slipped around the neck. The gas detection armband is clearly visible. The angled torch carried on the belt is a plastic American model. The trousers are standard 1937 Pattern issue. Group Captain Surplice, standing at left, presents Major General Gale with a tinx of treacle for his first breakfast on French soil.

Right: **Pathfinder officers are adjusting their watches before take off. Standing from left to right are Lieutenant Bobby de Latour, Lieutenant Don Wells, (the only one clad with the oversmock), Lieutenant John Fisher and Lieutenant Bob Midwood. All are equipped with US flashlights. Only Lieutenant De La tour carries a single magazine pouch for his sten, while Midwood, at left, has slipped his revolver into a tank crew type holster for easier access.**

58

Above: Random groups of para's have mustered for some rest after the previous night's combat. In the foreground, a Canadian para is recognizable by his khaki battledress trousers. His machine carbine is equiped with the fearsome spike bayonet for wich the weapon has been adapted by the addition of a bayonet lug. Next to him, two Bren machine-gunners are seen, the ammunition supplier carrying large bandoleers.

Right: A lance corporal and rifleman patrolling through the swamps, trying to recover the containers and their less-fortunate comrades.

Below: Sten Mark V at the ready, these two glider soldiers have taken cove behind a ditch near Benouville. As during the period, the picture shows the man at right wearing the Mark II helmet. One wonders if after 46 years, the roadsigns erected by the Germans to direct traffic to the centre of Caen are still be present.

Umgehung Caen-Nord

Umgehung Caen-Süd

CASUALTIES

Considering the circumstances of the battle and the difficulties involved in regrouping strayed soldiers trying to find the British lines, one is unable to assess the total amount of losses suffered by British paras during the night of 6 June.

By mid-July, Major General Gale estimated that the division's casualties stood at 2, 500 men including the losses suffered by an additional 600 volunteers drawn for non-airborne regiments.

On 1 September, 1944, at the end of the battle, casualties were established as follows:
- Wounded: 2, 709
- Killed: 821
- Missing in action: 927 [1]

Numbering 4, 457 men before the action, the 12th Batalion of the Parachute Regiment suffered the highest casualty rate, as they lost 105 men killed, 413 wounded, and 46 missing in action, out of a total of 613men.

1 : As 878 of these men were liberated in May 1945, 49 officers and other ranks must be considered as definitively lost.

The task of the 6th Airborne Brigade will be the occupation and defence of the Longueval-Sainte-Honorine-La Chardonette-Escoville-le Bas de Ranville sector

Finally, lord Lovat's 1st Special Service Brigade landed in the thre 3rd Infantry Division sector to urgently rejoin the 5th Parachute Brigade and deploy along the coastal zone between Franceville, Cabourg and Varaville.

The Battle

Asthis text does not cover every minutel detailof the battle, we recommend the following books :

The capture of intact bridges crossing th Orne canal and river is thoroughly dealt with 'Pegasus Bridge, June 1944', by Stephen Ambrose.

Right: Raised thumbs and victory signs show the indomitable spirit of these smiling paras. On this evening of 5 June, some among them even start to strike up the old traditional pub chant, its refrain being 'run, Rabit, run, Rabitt, run, run, run' a truly strange and outlandish sound at this time and place. Crowded together on the metal floor of a quad-engines Stirling Mark IV, modified to carry troops (RAF quadrons 190, 196, 299, and 620) they do not enjoy relative comfort some of their counterparts are enjoying in the 150 Dakotas. Next to the thighs of the medical sergeant in the foreground are a pair of woolen gloves, meant to protect the wearer against eventual scratches and grazes during the landing. The para in front (right) holds a large hot tea bottle, held in its own container, the contents are served at the first-aid stations. All men wear the parachutist trousers, the pockets of wich look to be amply stuffed. The oversmock worn under the parachute harness and life-jacket avoids equipment interfering with the opening of the parachute. The crew's faces are smeared with green camouflage ointment, appearing rather dull on this picture.

June, in the evening. The dynamic motto of the 6th Airborne, devised by Major General Gale himself while taking over command, will now earn its proper meaning.

At 22 h 56, at the RAF Tarrant Rushton airfield, six Horsa type gliders under the command of major Howard are taking off, towed by their large Halifax quad engines. Seven minutes later, at Harwell base, 60 Pathfinders belonging to the 22nd Independant Company of the army air corps are emptying their tea mugs, stub out their cigarettes, and haul themselves to the cabins of the six Albemarle twin-engined planes. They will form the spearhead of the immense armada constituted by the 38th and 46th Groups of the RAF Transport Command wich carries the main body of the 6th division. All base personnel not on duty is massed along the runways, shouting to show their support to the airborne troops, by now crowded together in their planes and gliders, trying to suppress their emotion, while at a short distance, a sizeable number of Waaf and Naafi personel stealthily wipe away an occasional tear. Suddenly, a flash lights up from the control tower. The pilot release the brakes, accelerate their engines to full throttle and leave the runways in rapid succession. The dice is cast!

The 6th Airborne Division

In May 1943, the 6th Airborne is officially formed in britain, and during the subsequent months, the various

Go to it!

Left: Though not redily apparent, these men are not infantry belonging to the airlanding brigade, but paratroopers joining their comrades, already in the field by 6 June. Burdened by heavy load, they have to rely on the assistance of a buddy to hoist themselves in the horsa's interior. At lefts an officer oversees the bording procedure, wearing his personnal equipment under his harness including his harness including officer's musette bag, and a lightweight gas mask hanging horizontally from his belt. Obviously, not any trooper is issued the special trousers. Standing between two medical corpsmen we note a despatch rider clad with the boots and helmet specific to his function, the latter closely ressembling the parachutist helmet.

THE 6th AIRBORNE DIVISION ON 6 JUNE 1944

HEADQUARTERS

6th Airborne Divisional Headquarter
- 317th Field Security Section
- Mobile Photo Enlargement Section
- Forward Observer Unit
- Chaplains (Royal Army Chaplain's Department)

6 AB Armoured Reconnaissance Regiment (Royal Armoured Corps)

6 AB Provost Company (Corps of Military Police)

22nd Airborne Para Company (Army Air Corps)

6 AB Postal unit (Royal Engineers)

6 AB Divisional Signals (Royal Corps of Signals)

Headquarter 3rd Para Brigade and defence platoon (Brigadier S.J.L Hill)
- 8th Battalion, Parachute Regiment
- 9th Battalion, Parachute Regiment
- 1st Canadian Parachute Battalion

Headquarter 5th Para Brigade and defence platoon (Brigadier J.H.N Poett)
- 7th Battalion, Parachute Regiment (light infantry)
- 12th Battalion, Parachute Regiment (Yorkshire)
- 13th Battalion, Parachute Regiment (Lancashire)

Headquarter 6th Airlanding Brigade and defence platoon (Brigadier H Kindersley)
- 12th Battalion Devonshire Regiment [1]
- 2nd Battalion Oxfordshire and Buckinghamshire Light Infantry
- 1st Battalion Royal Ulster Rifles

Headquarter 6th Airborne Divisional Artillery (Royal Artillery)
- 2nd Field Observer unit
- 211th-212th Airlanding light batteries
- 53rd Airlanding Light Regiment
- 2nd Airlanding light anti-aircraft battery
- 3rd Airlanding anti-tank battery
- 4th Airlanding anti-tank battery [2]

Headquarter 6th Airborne Divisional Engineers (Royal Engineers)
- 3rd Parachute Squadron
- 286th Field park company
- 591st Parachute Squadron
- 294th Field park company

Headquarter 6th Airborne Divisional Royal Army Service Corps
- 716th Airborne Light Company
- 398th Airborne divisional company [2]
- 63rd Airborne divisional company

Headquarter 6th Airborne Divisional Ordnance Royal Army Ordnance Corps
- Divisional Ordnance field park

Headquarter 6th Airborne Divisional Royal Army Electrical and Mechanical Engineers
- 6th Divisional workshop company [3]
- Airlanding Light Aid Detachment
- Airlanding Light Aid Detachment
- Airlanding Light Aid Detachment
- Airlanding Light Aid Detachment
- Airlanding Light Aid Detachment

Royal Army Medical Corps
- 195th Airlanding Field Ambulance
- 224th Airlanding Field Ambulance
- 225th Airlanding Field Ambulance

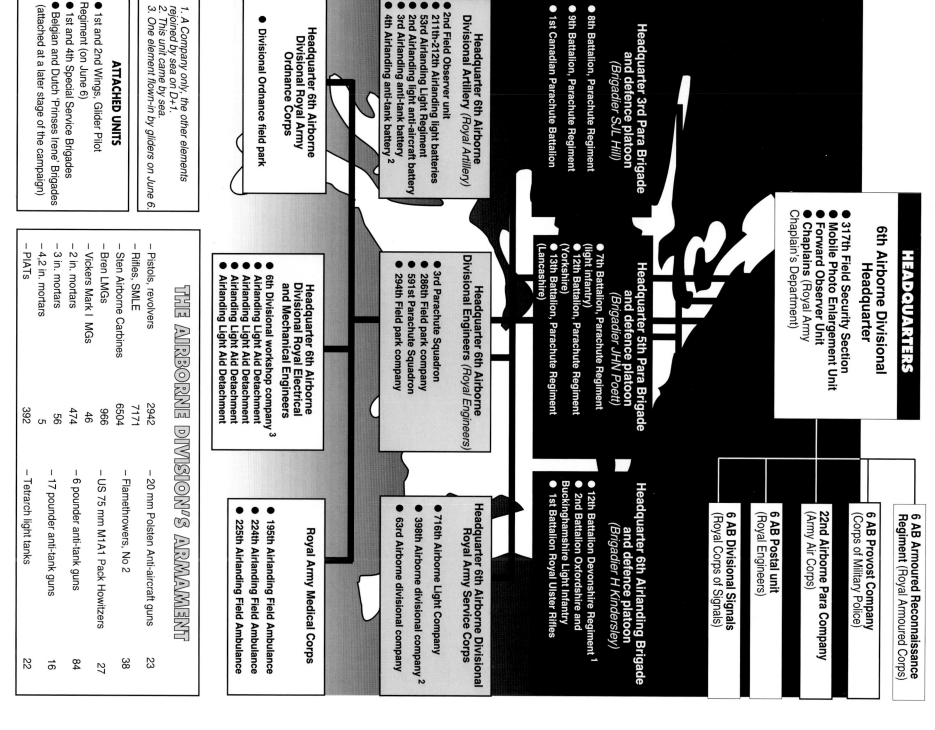

ATTACHED UNITS

- 1st and 2nd Wings, Glider Pilot Regiment (on June 6)
- 1st and 4th Special Service Brigades
- Belgian and Dutch 'Prinses Irene' Brigades (attached at a later stage of the campaign)

1. A Company only, the other elements rejoined by sea on D+1.
2. This unit came by sea.
3. One element flown-in by gliders on June 6.

THE AIRBORNE DIVISION'S ARMAMENT

Pistols, revolvers	2942
Rifles, SMLE	7171
Sten Airborne Carbines	6504
Bren LMGs	966
Vickers Mark I MGs	46
2 in. mortars	474
3 in. mortars	56
4.2 in. mortars	5
PIATs	392
20 mm Polsten Anti-aircraft guns	23
Flamethrowers, No 2	38
US 75 mm M1A1 Pack Howitzers	27
6 pounder anti-tank guns	84
17 pounder anti-tank guns	16
Tetrarch light tanks	22

THE PARATROOPERS' UNIFORMS

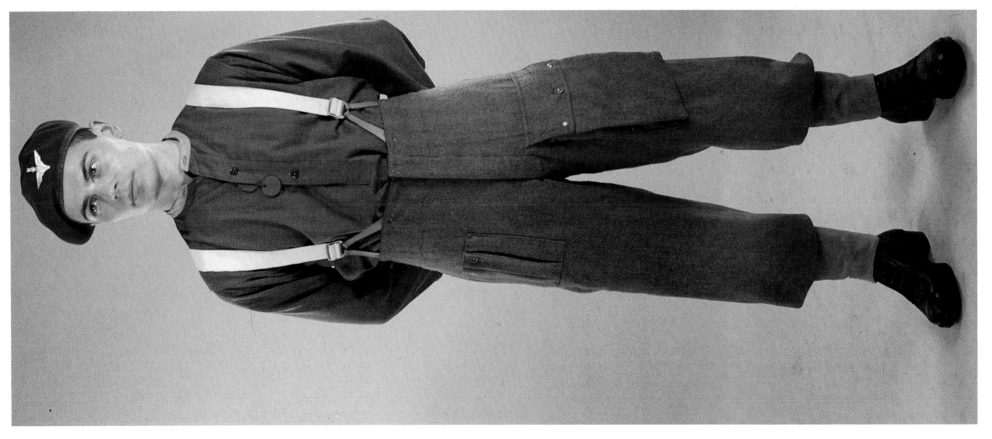

The Legendary Maroon Beret

Shortly before raising the parachute regiment in August 1942 by blending the already existing battalions, the commander of the airborne forces, Major General Browning, opted for the adoption of a distinctive type of headwear. The airborne pattern chosen will be a woollen beret identical to the one worn by the Royal Armoured Corps. The General Staff of the 1st Airborne Division will be offered the choice of two shades: maroon and light blue. Two enlisted men will be appointed to display the proposed models.

The choice will be the maroon version though it seems the final decision was not easily reached. While the officials in charge of the agreement were still tied up with endless arguing, the story persists that one of the soldiers displaying one of the models strongly advocated the adoption of the maroon beret, wich consequently won the approval of all parties. Psychologically, it was to be a master stroke. In fact, nothing more could express the unit morale of these warriors, a large amount of these having a working class background, to affirm their prestige toward the civilian population and moreover vis a vis the other armed branches. Officially approved 29 July, 1942, the beret, airborne, will undergo its baptism of fire with the 1st Airborne Brigade during Operation Torch in November 1942. The maroon beret will be worn by all personnel concurrently with all dress types, unless the wear of the helmet is ordered. In fact, even tank crews of the 6th Airborne Reconaissance Regiment switched their black beret in favor of the maroon ones. The beret is to be worn showing the cap badge of the regiment or corps to which the owner belongs.

The Typical Uniform

Altough complex in appearance, the dress items designed for the paras are simple in their use, their primary function being to allow the minimum loss of body heat during air transport and actual descent without hampering movement after reaching the ground. After some experimentation with jump suits quite sqimilar to their German counterparts, the year 1941 will see the introduction of the Denison smock, named after its designer Major Denison. Finally it will be decided to equip the paras with two distinctive garments: a sleeveless jump blouse, (see next chapter) to be discarded after landing, and a camouflage blouse to be worn underneath the former over the standard issue woollen dress. The Denison smock should provide thermal isolation during drops as well as an adequate camouflage in the field. As these qualities are of prime importance to all airborne troops, the smock will be distributed to the glider staff as well as to the parachutists.

The Shirt

The standard issue army shirt (angola shirt) is tailored from brown flannel. The collarless shirt is lined with khaki cotton. It is quite long, especially at the rear. Afront opening runs midway down the chest. All buttons were made of metal are cupped stampings, inclded the cuff ones.

Right: **This Parachute Regiment Lance-Corporal displays the typical parachutist uniform, the main item being the special trousers, easily identified by their extra capacity side pocket. Its front opening, being of a particular design, is closed by buttons and snap fasteners. The braces , footwear and leggings are standard issue. Hanging around the neck is a set of pressed cardboard identification tags. According to regulations, the cap badge is to be worn above the left eye.**

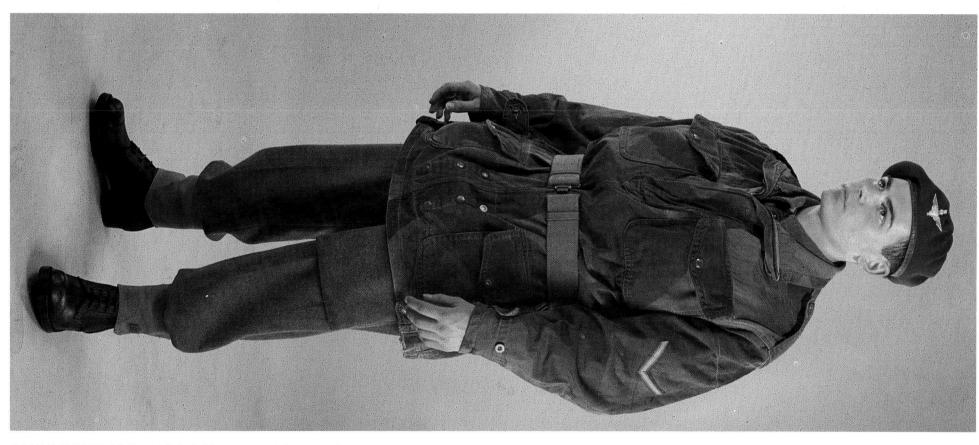

Above: This Denison smock features a modification to the flap passing between the legs. When not used it gets simply fastened to the rear of the smock. The 'brushstroke' camouflage pattern is clearly shown.

Left: This soldier, outfitted with the complete uniform is wearing a 2nd type Denison smock over the standard battledress, the former having buttoned cuffs. Typical reference points for the Denison smock are: the turn down collar fitted with a zipper down to mid chest, the buttoned shoulder straps, the waist adjustment tabs fastened with snap fasteners and the four large pockets with snapped down pocket flaps. At the front skirt, three pairs of snap fasteners are placed to t fasten the flap running between the legs. The sole insignia worn on the smock are the rank and qualification badges.

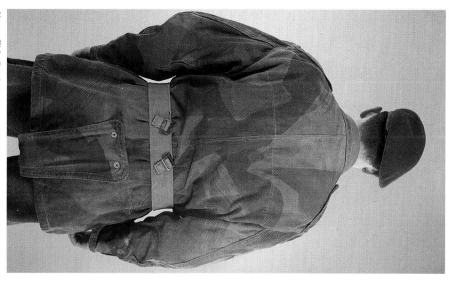

The Denison Smock

Consists of a blouse made of sturdy camouflage patterned cotton twill, non reversible and amply sized. The cotton fabric used, ensuring adequate protection against the wind but not water repellent. The camouflage pattern gives the illusion of of being roughly applied by dark green and chocolate brown brush strokes on a light green background. The shades may vary from one manufacturer to another and by wear.

The smock is pulled over the head, and sealed by a concealed front zipper running from the chin down to the chest. On certain smocks, the zipper is replaced with brass or plastic buttons passing through cloth loops. On the chest, two horizontally placed inside pockets similar to these on the woollen blouse are provided. The sleeves have elasticated knitwear cuffs.

In addition, the sleeves have six ventilation eyelets at armpit level. Two small adjustment tabs are stitched on both sides of the lower skirt, held down by snap fasteners for a comfortable fit at the waist. The simple collar is lined with a strip of brown flannel, and can either be zipped up or worn open. To keep the oversmock from 'creeing up' towards the armpits, a large flap has been provided for securing between the legs, and snap fastened to the lower front. Three pairs of snap fasteners ensure adjustment to the appropriate position. Introduced later in the war, the 2nd type Denison smock lacks the knitted cuffs, in this case, the sleeves were

1 - first model Denison smock vfitted with knitted cuffs, the type mostly worn in Normandy. The front zipper is made of iron. The camouflage colours are evident on thi well-preserved smock. The flannel band stitched in the collar's interior not withstanding, this smock is totally unlined. the manufacturer's label is affixed in the waist area, the metal snap fasteners are machine applied.

2 - Second model Denison smock having adjustment tabs at the cuffs, the zipper being made of brass.

3 - Parachute trousers. Seen from the rear, the two first aid pockets are exposed as well as the one on the tigh. Two buttons stitched at the waist-level allow the trousers to be attached to the woollen blouse. The manufacturer's label is affixed in the hollow of the back panel. At right, the dagger retaining pocket is shown. the austerly made braces are completely made from twill.

4 - parachute trousers. Lined with khaki twill and fitted with iron buttons for attaching the braces. The tight pocket, having lateral access permits thez carry of several items. At left, the dagger pocket with its two snaps fasteners and button holding the dagger sheath. The braces are made of twill and leather.

5 - Maroon beret (beret, airborne)

Two blackened ventilation holes are present, it is lined by black cotton. Through the leather head band runs a rayon string, having a knot at the rear. The manufacturers and quartermaster markings are stamped with white ink.

6 - String vest
At left, the wholly knitted type, at right, the one fitted with white cotton shoulder bands.

The Paratroopers' Uniform

to be tightened at the fore-arm by buttoned straps, allowing to positions. Numerous Denison smock variants are eseen, the style of the flap making the main difference. In actual field use, the flap tends to be an awkward addition and therefore is frequently cut off by the paras, only too glad to be rid of the 'ape tail'. Consequently, some smocks are manufactured with fully removable flaps, while others have back panels with snap fasteners providing the option of wearing the smock with the flap folded up to the rear, and out of the way when its function became useless after the jump.Occasionally, used woollen socks are found stitched together around the lower sleeves on smocks lacking elastic ated knitwear cuffs. To allow a speedier way of access, the mid-length zippers are sometimes replaced with full length zippers taken from the oversmock.

The Airborne Trousers

To complete the battledress blouse, a new uniform item exclusively designed for airborne use will be intro-

64

The String Vest

Looking like a mesh waistcoat, this peculiar issue garment has always been controversed.

Today, we know, from evidence provided by veterans and official sources, that it was not an 'invasion vest' but merely meant to retain body warmth by the reliable expedient of applying several layers of clothing on top of each other. This sleeveless vest, made of loosely woven white cotton string vest, was to become standard British Army issue. In cold weather, it was intended to be worn under or above the shirt whether one desired to increase or decrease body warmth.

The string vest was issued to all personnel along with the shirt and issue pullover, the wollen overcoat howe-

duced starting 1943 and known as: 'trousers, parachutist. However, on 6 June, many parachute batallions had not been issued with the new garment and therefore still wore the standard issue trousers.

The new pattern is very similar to the former but for some alterations, notably adapted for airborne duty. Its side pocket has bellowed gussets to allow extra room, it is closed by a rectangular flap thnaks to a central stitched button and two small brass keepers, snapped down at each end. Three pockets contain first-aid dressings,one rectangularly placed on the right front, and two more in each back pocket.

The fob watch pocket lacks the buttoned flap. A pocket with vertical slit to receive a sheated Fairbaim-Sykes dagger ison the right thigh, it closes by two snap fasteners when empty, and a plastic button is sewn to allow the upper part of the sheath to be secured. The large side pocket situated on the tigh and the two regular side pockets are buckskin lined, protecting the wearer against injury by sharp edged items.

Later models will have pockets lined with a sturdy, white twill. Lacking belt loops, the trousers should be worn with standard braces fastened by metal buttons. Among trousers in the possession of collectors, we found out that two kinds of fabric exist, one identical to the battledress, the second being more rigid and of the thicker variety used for the manufacture of the overcoats.

Left: Basically, the Denison smock is always worn over the woollen blouse, providing a certain amount of body heat and protecting against the wind. Shown here is a smock where, during manufacture, the zipper was replaced by six buttons and loops, these buttons made either of plastic, or ashere, brass. The helmet, a Mark I, has a rounded stainless shell. The stitching marks of the inner pockets can be seen right on top of the chest pockets.

Right: A paratroop second lieutnant wearing the combat uniform.The Denison smock is custom modified by his tailor who installed a full-length zipper to enable faster access. Other alterations observed on officer's smock consist of: overall lining, slanted pockets and knitwear cuffs. The parachute wings are sewn on the left arm, and second lieutenant pips adorn the shoulder straps, the former having a 'Cambridge blue' background, the Army Air Corps branch colour, to wich his regiment belongs. The open collar of the blouse reveals the shirt and tie. Equipment is composed of a belt to wich a web holster holding a Colt model 1911 automatic pistol and a web compass pouch is attached. At left, the snapped down partitioned pockets wich could contain the magazine for the FN HP Browning. A lanyard passing around the belt keeps the pistol from being lost. The individual weapon is the Sten Mark V machine carbine, its magazine being stuffed in the blouse pockets. Regulation N° 2 mark III binoculars are slung around the neck, its burdensome case left at the barracks. The parachute trousers are tucked into his leggings. His brown peibled leather shoes are of the high quality pattern reserved for officers' use, a variant is shown here having reinforced tips and straps. □

Footwear

After the temporary distribution of rubber-soled shoes, the standard ankle-boots were reintroduced, as there were actually no drawbacks encountered when using the hobnailed boots during or after the drop. Cotton leggings were secured around the ankles by two straps of web or leather. Their wear reduced rubbing of the trousers legs and protected them against wear.

Interestingly, some contemporary pictures show cadre and other mnks wearing the tall boots of the despatch riders, this particular service having its own pattern.

ver, was not included to reduce weight.

PARACHUTE CLOTHING AND EQUIPMENT

The Oversmock, Parachutist, 42 Pattern

This garment follows the initial jump blouse which was similar to the 'Falschirmjäger' pattern, and also had to serve as a combat dress. The latter, not being very suitable for ground combat, was refined and improved, the result to be introduced in 1942. Its role was to cover the equipment and the Denison smock during the the drop, reducing bulk and air resistance, and finally to ensure the correct opening of the parachute, shielding it against protruding equipment items.

Contemporary documents show that the not all paratroopers wore oversmocks in Normandy, the reason probably was to gain time after touch down. Distributed shortly before the start of 'Overlord', the oversmock was a long and sleeveless waistcoat, made from the same green cotton twill as used for the combat uniform of the British armed forces (the famous 'Denim'). From collar to bottom, a heavy duty zipper was installed, in a slightly slanting direction. This zipper enabled the oversmock to be shed in a matter of seconds. The collar was identical to that of the Denison smock, and identically lined with a strip of brown flannel. To ensure its correct fit during descent, and provide an easy way to allow the placement of the harness straps of the parachute, a flap was used which passes between the legs and was fixed at the back by means of snap fasteners. Two small pockets were alternatively placed next to the zipper, their opening secured by an elastic band. These were often used for holding Mills grenades, these being carried along to ward off opposition on the ground. We also notice that the smock has no shoulders straps.

The Leg Bag

Introduced in earlyf 1943, the leg bag like all specially designed individual and collective equipment has two purposes (see the weapons chapter). When creating parachute units, it was considered vital that the soldier should land without his gear and armament so they would not interfere with his movements during the des-

Above right: **Led by a stick leader, a group of paracTROOPER prepare to board the Albemarle standing ready to take off. On the runway, the men are cheked and giving achalk mark to signify the all-clear mark. Individual equipment is, shown by the presence of the spike bayonet and canteen, when, the oversmock is not worn. The first two men in the row carry their cumbersome haversacks on their stomachs. The ubiquitous dagger is seen in the thigh pocket of the stick leader's parachute trousers.**

Left: **A British paratrooper in complete jump suit. Besides the placement of the harness straps running over the life jaket and the oversmock, we notice the way the rope of the leg bag is fixed to one of the straps. This NCO's leg bag contains his equipment and regulation issue weapon, a Sten mark V machine carbine. A large field shovel handle is seen protruding from the bag.**

Above: the leg bag is tightly secured to the leg by two straps, one beneath the knee and one at the ankle. A pocket stitched at the bag's rear contain the unbuckling device. The oversmock covers the whole of the equipment, so as to keep edges or bumps from interfering with the opening of the parachute. For hand protection a mere pair of regulation woollen gloves was deemed sufficient.

Left: **A gas armband is worn around the left sleeve. The parachute main bag is by a drawstring meant to be severed by the tension of the static line. The string can be seen coiled on the bag. At left we note a white twill label, bearing the parachute's specifications and manufacture origin. The soldier's right hand holds a device which serves to slow down the leg bag's descent. Its rope which connects the bag to the harness is coiled in the vertical slit stitched on the side where the disconnecting device is also housed.**

cent. Therefore, it was initially thought that the equipment would be dropped separatly in specially designed containers evolved around that time. During exercises which followed, it soon became clear that it was very difficult, especially at night, for the men to recover the containers. Since this separation of men and their 'tools of the trade' resulting from this practice could obviously not be accepted, further to design special containers which could accompany the para during the descent.

This function was fulfilled by the leg bag, containing the individual equipment and small arms such as Sten mark V machine carbine or various other gear considered necessary to complete the mission. For the attack in Normandy, a considerable amount of material had to be carried (ammunition, transmitters, signalling gear). Evidence shows that, the mode of charging the leg bag was left to each individual. While some jumped with leg bags containing a complete set of equipment, others opted to take along the most essential part of the 1937

Parachute clothing and equipment

Above: Superimposed on this oversmock showing its manufacturer's label and fitted with a flannel collar, are two rubber life-jackets and at right, a leg bag. The method of securing is clearly shown: two straps have buckles for tightening around the leg, and held in place by two keepers. Unfastening is activated by tearing a white tape stitched to the top of the bag. A leather strap holding the recovery system is covered by a snap fastened heavy canvas flap, to accidental deployment. The space for the foot at the bottom of the bag is clearly shown. The fixing of the bag cord to the harness is provided by a snap hook.

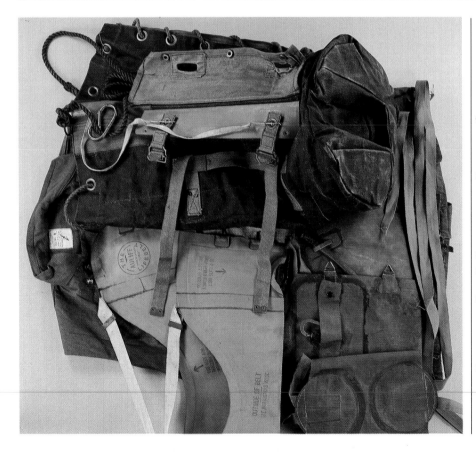

Below: Last moments before to taking off. The parachute-qualified medic at left bears the haversack and folded poncho. His personal tool and gas mask are held by a string. The parachute harness seems to be brown. A pair of bandage scissors are tucked in the leg dagger pocket. Attached to an airborne medical unit, the padre at right has the cap badge of a catholic chaplain pinned to his beret, as well as pips denoting his rank embroidered on a purple background, this being the service colour of the Army Chaplain Department. All members of this branch are officers. Both wear red cross armbands.

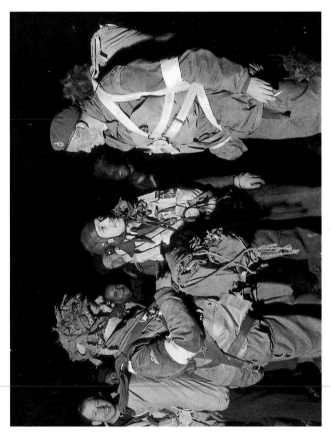

Above: A Pattern 1942 oversmock, looking very much like its German counterpart. A piece of string is attached to the zipper for better grip. As a matter of fact the smock was shed in the shortest possible time after touchdown so as to reach the equipment faster. The flap between the legs was held to the smock's front by four snap fasteners. Right : a smoke grenade is carried in one of the small front pockets.

equipment, the latter only stuffed under their buckled harness. Extra care was given to the sailing bag, its weight increasing the stability of the body during the jump. Made from a strong cotton twill, the bag was amply padded at the bottom, a rectangular cavity was provided to accommodate the foot. To facilitate the opening of the bag after the jump, a long slit was cut on the outside, sealed by lacing a cord from top to bottom through sets of eyelets placed on each side of the slit. During transport, the bag was secured to the leg by a system of quick release straps, and loosened shortly before touchdown. At this moment, the bag was no longer secured to the harness, but was hanging from a long strop uncoiled on command by the parachutist with the aid of a friction handle.

The Life Jacket

Distributed to all 6th Airborne personnel before the landing, the life jacket was carried in the cargo planes as well as in the gliders. It was designed for airborne use. Made of greyish or greenish rubber, it was worn around the chest. Four cotton straps were stitched on its back, two at the top and another two at waist level. The top ones passed over the shoulders to keep the garment in place. The lower straps were slipped between the legs and crossed the chest through triangulars rings, before being fastened with a simple knot to ensure adequate fit on the chest. Apparently, these straps were worn relatively slack to enable inflating and not interfere with the bearer's movements. Inflating was achieved by activating two small CO_2 cartridges, pla-

Above: **A good example showing the placement of individual equipment when the leg bag was not taken used. The** suspension system (belt and pouches, bayonet and canteen) is displayed in the conventional fashion. The individual tool and lightweight gas mask being secured to the haversack held by a strap around the waist. The dagger visible in its special pocket was only meant for close-combat, and not to severe the harness straps, as these were automatically unbuckled by a device carried at mid-chest. Sometimes, a Sten Mark V with buttstock removed was fixed to the chest by the harness straps.

ced at the front on each side of the jacket. The CO^2 cartridges were set off by a small toggle. Additional inflating could be obtained by blowing through a rubber mouthpipe placed at left in the jacket's interior.

When surveying a complete parachute equipment, we notice that it consists of a Denison smock, personal gear, oversmock, life jacket, parachute harness and including the leg bag, the latter being ommitted by men issued with a Lee Enfield or Bren as these weapons had their own specially designed carrier cases. □

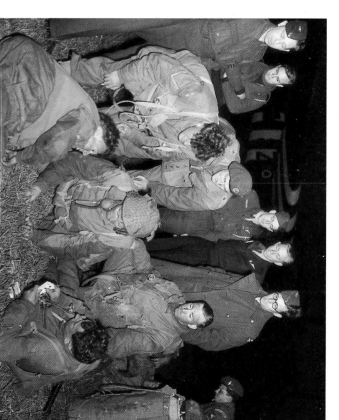

Above: The evening of 5 June: paratroopers enjoy a game of cards, watched by bystanders. This picture was taken at the same base as shown on page 30. According to the cap badge worn by the man at center, this group belongs to the Pathfinders of the 22nd Independant Company of the Army Air Corps, scheduled to take off at 11 o'clock. Their leg bags can be seen on the ground at right, each one bearing its owner's name. A helmet and a few Sten magazines lie on the left leg bag which probably holds a Rebecca wireless set. Behind the man slumping at right in the grass, we notice a Sten Mark II S equipped with a silencer and further typified by its pistol grip and canvas barrel shroud, here barely recognizable. This weapon was used for operations demanding utmost discretion. Further to be noticed is the way the life jacket is secured. Each man wears an oversmock.

Right: **A corporal with opened leg-bag. Its weight exceeded 45 kg during the the Normandy attack. The** indispensable face veil, normally provided for camouflage, is used as a scarf here. The toggle rope is held in the prescribed manner. One of the chest pocket holds a US type TL 122 A angled flashlight replacing the familiar British issue torch. Two web ammunition pouches, of the lerger type hold the machine carbine magazines.

The X-Type Parachute

By Yves Tariel

Only after the war was declared did the British decide to design a parachute to equip their newly raised airborne. At that time the only parachute in use was that issued to air crews, and activated after leaving the aircraft.

No previous studies were undertaken concerning the use of a parachute as a means of delivering troop. Let us take a closer look at the static line opening type X 'Statichute' already devised by the British.

Initially, this parachute was designed in 1936 by Raymond Quilter and James Gregory, founders of the GQ parachute company, who consequently offered their findings to the British officials. Their endeavours were motivated by the advance already made by the German with their RZ parachute, fitted with a static line opening system. The GQ patent incorporated the canopy design of the Irvin parachute, the latter being used as a starting point to develop the 'statichute'.

At this time, the War Office was not yet considering the creation of an airborne force, thus Quilter when offe-

ring his advice, was politely sent back to his workshop.

In 1940, impressed by the victories of German paratroopers, Churchill insisted on creating airborne forces. Back then, though, the massive drop of troops was still an unwritten chapter, the only chapter, the only British experience thustar consisting of a few rescue jumps executed by air crews. These were to be further tested and the findings used to develop a strategy to adapt

the use of parachutes for airborne combat resulting in the raising of appropriate units. Due 'however' to the meagre experience, some problems seemed insurmountable, severly aggravated by the understandable reluctance encountered when trying to round up the necessary volunteers who would perform the risky tests.

Meanwhile, the War Office, aware there were differents way of approaching the problem that started to look for a more delicate way to enlist personnel to jump. Accordingly, the Central Landing Establishment was born, and reluctant at first, one by one volunteers started to trickle in.

Still, the RAF rescue parachutes with delayed opening were kept for use. After 57 of these 'delayed opening' jumps had been made at the new training grounds, one of the parachutes refused to open, causing the death of a trainee

Immediately, all training was postponed, as the further utilisation of the delayed opening system was deemed too dangerous and not to be continued. A change-over to a system doing away with the static line opening was undertaken by attaching a strap to the plane wich had to activate the opening of the bag and deployment of the canopy.

So, the Quilter and gregory 'Statichute' was reconsidered resulting in the birth of the British army parachute, commonly known as the X-Type.

T5 versus X-Type

It would be interesting to briefly compare the X-type with the parachute used by the American paratroopers at the same era. The T3 and T5 (described in Militaria 22/23) employed a peculiar mode of deployment. They were triggered by the traction of the static line affixed on top of the canopy, followed by the suspension lines. On the X-type, however the sequence was reversed. One and a half second after leaving the plane, the bag opened and released the canopy bag, from which the suspension lines were first extracted before the canopy deployed. The breakable string on the canopy snapped while the static line and canopy bag stayed attached to the plane. The characteristic impact at the opening of the American type parachute was seriously lessened on the X-type, and risk of mixing up the suspension lines were also diminished. In the first place, the new technique allowed for simplified training of the parachutrooper as the harshness of the jump was considerably softened. Also, it allowed for low altitude openings, reducing the scattering of troops after landing. In wartime, the life-span of the X-type was considered to be 25 jumps. Maintenance and rigging was cared for by the female RAF auxilliaries, the WAAF.

Description

The 'Statichute' or X-type is made up of four main components: the canopy, the harness, the canopy bag with automatic opening strap (static line) and the container bag shielded by its four flaps.

The Canopy

The canopy, being the main element, is not so rounded as modern parachutes. Its diameter is 8,55 metres. Initially made of silk, it was mass produced during the war from a special cotton fabric known as Ramex. An opening was present at the upper part to ensure stability during the descent. This circular opening, called apex, mesures 55 centimetres across, and is made of heavy duty Ramex, more resistant and porous than the canopy. It further consists of 28 cells reinforced by a framework of 28 suspension lines converging to the canopy. All suspensions lines cross at the apex on top of the crown. They are either made from silk or rayon, depending on the model and year of manufacture. The 28 suspension lines converging to the harness are divided in four groups of seven, attached to elevators, (straps departing from the parachutist's shoulder towards the canopy) by means of metal fittings.

The harness is formed by a set of straps keeping the jumper attached to the parachute. These straps join the right set of suspension lines, the left set passing under the seat of the user, by forming a 'U' where he actually sits. It is the harness main part.

It is further completed by two straps parting from each shoulder to pass over the chest, then converging at the stomach and going all the way to the rear. Two others, called thigh straps, part from the 'U's interior and part join at the stomach after passing under each branch of the 'U'. The four straps converging to the stomach are then buckled by small metal fittings held in a central housing containing a quick release device securing the complete set. To conclude, an X-shaped strap connects the dorsal bag with its four flaps, holding the canopy, the suspension lines, canopy bag and static line on the parachute back.

The load capacity of one single harness amounts to 1,300 kilos. The 'U' shaped main strap consists of four regular straps having a load capacity of 200 kilos each.

The Canopy Bag and Static Line

The bag is conceived to contain the folded canopy and the suspension lines. Made of heavy duty canvas, it is rectangularly shaped, and opens at one of its extremities. To protect the folded canopy, the flap cover is fastened up at each corner by an elastic band through which pass the first braid of the suspension lines. The full length of the suspension lines is coiled on the bag by means of of other similar rubber bands, or twill loops, depending on the model.

On the other extremity of the bag, a static line is stitched onto the robust reinforcements made of the same kind of bands. The extremity of the static line ends up in twill rig which passes through the interior of the canopy bag. This ring is designed to be attached on top of the folded canopy by means of a string which snaps when a tension of 50 kilos is applied. During the drop, the string will be severed by rupture at the moment when the tension of the static line detaches the paratrooper from the plane. At this moment, the canopy, already extracted from its bag starts shaping up to finally deploy.

The Parachute Bag

The parachute bag is secured to the paratrooper's back by two crossing harness straps.
Its function is to contain the canopy and canopy bag.

The X-type admirably served throughout World War 2, ending its carreer in its original version with the French-British expedition during the 1956 Suez crisis. During this conflict, it was realized that the X-type began to show serious signs of obsolescence especially when compared to the excellent French TAP 660 parachute.

Consequently it underwent some minor modifications: it became less bulky and was at last coupled with a re'serve parachute secured to the stomach. Constantly improved over the years it is still in use today and known as the PXI Mk 4.

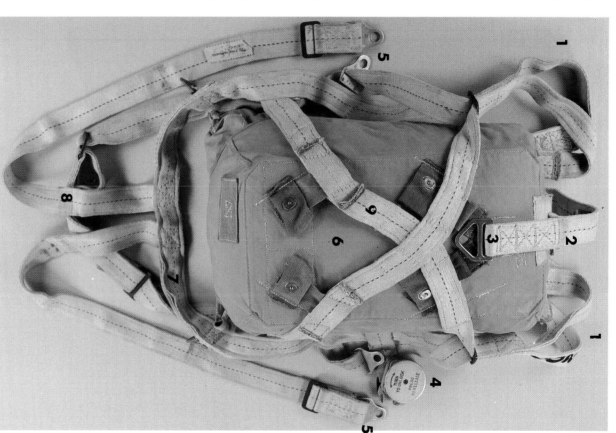

The X-Type Mk II Parachute

1 - elevator
2 - static line
3 - static line extension fixing point
4 - connection and quick-release housing
5 - connection and quick-release buckles
6 - main bag
7 - butt strap, the harness's main part
8 - thigh straps
9 - dorsal straps sustaining the main bag extending the straps at the chest (normally, these are slipped through the straps in staggered rows)

The bag is made of four flaps maintained by a string, which will snap if a pulling force of 25 kilos occurs. The elevators joining the canopy to the harness protrude from the bag at shoulder level. The static line protrudes at the point of convergence of the four straps and is vertically coiled either at the bag's exterior in two small canvas pockets, this in case of the Mark II model, as on the Mark II the strap lies coiled partially inside.

The parachute is now ready for employment as soon as the static line is hooked on its extension inside the aircraft's fuselage. Should this be overlooked, the careless paratrooper will then be lost beyond hope, as the X-Type, similar to the German RZ is not coupled with a reserve parachute.

PARATROOPER'S COMBAT UNIFORM

Due to strong gales, the Pathfinders only partially succeed marking the dropping zones of the 3rd and 5th para brigades consequently dispersed all over the coast. Once rid of his parachute and jump blouse, paratrooper has to hasten adjusting his equipment, starting with the content of the leg bag, take off the cover of his individual weapon, followed by the search for his fellows and the containers holding the necessary items to complete the mission. Several times during the night, the reassuring password and rallying signal is heard, being 'V for Victory', made to all personnels prior to the landing, it was spoken or whistled using the morse code: three shorts sounds, followed by a stretched one. Some units were known to assemble by the sound of a hun-

Left: 6 June, at dawn, the corporal at left has discarded his Sten machine carbine in favor of the group's Bren machine gun, which previous gunner and loader are out of combat. Besides the weapon, he is bearing pouches holding th Bren gun magazines as well as a small cleaning kit held by a canvas pouch attached at the bandoleer seen at right. Only the special trousers and sleeve insignia show that he belongs to an airborne battalion. Due to high temperature on this sunny moring, the blouse's collar is left open, revealing the camo veil around around the neck, normally used to hide the face in case of sniper fire. A Hawkins anti-tanks mine is hidden in the left pocket of the Denison smock and a Mills defensive grenade hooked by its lever to the belt. The red beret, the paratrooper most coveted equipment item is rolled up in the left pocket.

Above: 10 June, 1944, between Amfreville and Ranville. Mistakenly dropped too far from their assigned landing job, these paras of the 12th battalion have seen a lot of combat while wandering three days behind ennemy lines. They give a cheerful 'thumbs-up' to display their joy when British lines were at last reached. Others are eagerly opening beef and sausage tins. The man, standing at the extreme left has removed his leggings, obviously to dry his trousers after the walk through the swamps. The man next to him wears a leather model 1903 belt buckle adorned with a menacing Colt model 1911 automatic pistol, these being the only remaining items of his initial equipment. The ammunition for the rifle, whose spike bayonet is fixed on the muzzle, is carried in lightweight twill bandoleer. The man at left has successfully concealed the shape of his helmet by applying his face veil.

ting horn or a bird call. By morning the majority of objectives will be reached and secured untill more reinforcements will arrive by ship. Before this could happen, the objectives were defiantly defended by the German garrisons. Contrary to their American counterparts, the 82nd and 101st Airborne, the British airborne forces will pursue ground ground combat at the Normandy front untill August.

Right: Shown here is paratrooper outfitted according to regulations. Due to chastic battle conditions, the full equipment worn prior to the jump is seldom observed on period photographs. The haversack worn on the back with the adjustable straps, hooked above the pouches, contains the canteen, eating utensils, shoes, underwear and toileteries. The poncho ground sheet is neatly folded. The field shovel, notably more efficient than the folding entreching tool is stuck under the haversack, the latter holding the spade. The man's tool, hanging in its web case also containing its handle, is fixed to his back. The toggle rope is ready for use, we note its buckling system. The Denison smock buttflap, now useless, is snap-fastened to the rear.

THE AIRLANDING BRIGADE

THE GLIDER BATALLIONS are regular army units duly appointed to the Glider Division, unlike to the Parachute battalions totally made-up of volunteers

Considering the risks involved when serving in the gliders, a way out was foreseen, by leaving the appointees to transfer to other branches, though few take the opportunity. In contrast with their 'Dardevil' counterpart, the gliders infantrymen offering the reassuring and earnest image of the career army[1].

These battalions, drawn from either the light infantry regiment or the Rifles were hardened veterans units baseded in India, before being ordered back to home-

Below: 6 June, a Horsa having completed his journey by crashing into a wall. The open front door doubles as a ramp to unload a motorcycle. Clearly seen are the various patriotic inscriptions on the fuselage.

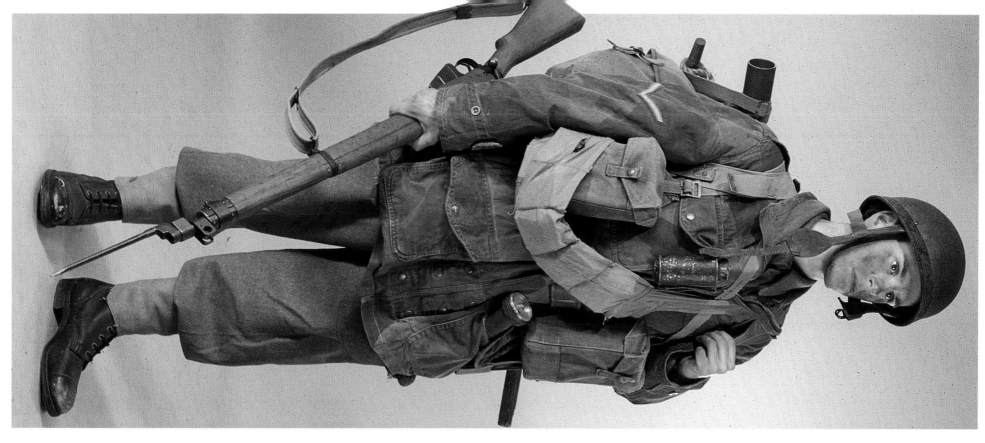

The glider fusilier totes a notable heavier load than the paraTROOPER. A SMLE N°4 Mark I with fixed spike bayonet arms this lance corporal. Two lightweight webb pouches fixed to his belt hold his ammunitions supply. The basic pouches contains rifle clips and mortar grenades, a smoke grenade is attached by its lever to the smock's chest pocket and one of his inner pocket holds a flash light. The uniform is identical to the one issued to the parachustists except for the trousers, these being here the standard army version with their plated thigh pocket and single pocket for the first aid dressing. Already considerably outfitted, a Berghaus mountain rucksack is added to the load, a model commonly issued to British assault troops. The rucksack is fitted with metal frame. It contains among other personal gear and issue items, food rations and ammunitions, a folded poncho/ground sheet and rope. Furthermore added-on straps parmit a small two inch mortar to be stowed on top. To complete the load, a green canvas gas-maskbag is hung over his chest.

land to receive the particular training adapted to their new mission. They are to undergo combat training in the hills of Wales before joining the Airborne Division in october 1941. Their number and armament will be superior to those of the paratroopers. ❑

1. Not totally overshadowing the differences in temperament between the British and the hot tempered Irish of the Royal Ulster Rifles.

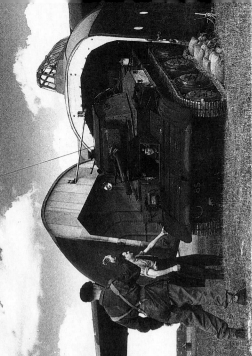

GLIDER PILOTS

IN 1941, the glider pilot regiment will be raised, to be commanded by major Chatterton, an ex-fighter pilot. To man the new unit, volunteers will be drawn from the army. Required to hold the sergeant rank at least recruits will be withhold able to pass the rigorous physical and psychological tests. The pilot school will be run by the RAF, the basic glider training by the army.

The Glider Pilot Helmet

(By Marcus Cotton).

The philosophy behind the establishment of the airborne forces require that the majority of the troops should be transported by gliders planes, the remaining 10% too be dropped by parachute.

The glider pilot regiment will consist of army pilots. They will be trained in various sites erected at the exercice grounds of Salisbury, such as Bulford and Netheravon. Many pilots will graduate there during the fall of 1942.

Above: **At Ranville, Major General Gale's glider lying taken down in a field. We note the cylindrical diameter of the fuselage and the bolts placed on its contour, allowing a speedy separation of the nose for unloading. The passengers are sitting face-to-face.**

Below: **The fusiliers belonging to second wave are comparing their artistic talents. The company quartermaster sergeant holding the piece of chalk has his dagger fixed on his trouser's leg by two buttoned loops. On top : a glider pilot equipped with his special helmet and RAF Goggles. A bayonet is laying one of the suspension straps, the owner being the soldier standing on the boarding steps.**

The Helmet, Crash, Glider Pilot

As a matter of fact, a shock absorbing helmet will be needed for the pilots, due to harsh landing conditions the gliders planes are bound to endure. By reason of its weight, the parachutist helmet is unsuitable, and further by the fact that they can only be fitted with regular headliners unable to allow space for the headsets needed for communication between the tOWING plane and the glider plane. Thus, a suitable helmet will be designed providing the solution to these problems. Meanwhile, unmodified fibre motorcycle helmet will be used for training purposes. By september 1942, training helmets expressly for glider pilots will be delivered to the RAF. These are in fact fibre motorcycle helmet with leather 'C' type headliners installed. Another model is observed made up by the modification of of motorcycle helmets issued to despatch riders and civilian fire departments.

The definitive version will be manufactured from riveted fibre parts, covered by canvas which is fireproofed with a layer of special paint. Being more compact, they are still fitted with the lower part of the 'C' type headliners. Since they were conceived and supplied by the air force, the amount needed will have to be ordered from the air ministry. Consequently, each helmet will bear the latter's ink stamp designing the air ministry catalog number and size : 22c/941 for the smallest size (6 3/4) to 22c/947 for size 7 1/2.

On 1 July 1943, the army orders hits helmets. For the years 1943 and 1944, respectively 2,600 and 1,740 pieces. Six hundred helmets will be needed to equip Glider Pilot regiment, and as by the aforementioned date 351 are already in stock, the balance will have to reach the unit by the next two weeks.

Following the raising of more pilot units, 4,040 more helmets are ordered, bringing the amount to 5,870 pieces by 1944. The helmet, crash, glider pilot will be outdated october 2nd, 1953.It should be pointed out, however, that the glider pilots as well as the crew received paratroops helmet in addition of their own shock absorbing models.

The Horsa Glider

After the failure with the 'Hotspur', the Airspeed company is approached in January, 1941 to design a towaircraft. In September a test flight will be undertaken, followed by regular production in June 1942. The Horsa is able to haul 29 men and motorcycles (with or without their side-cars). When lowered, the side-door with special designed hinges, functions as a loading and unloading ramp, assisted by two hollow support rails, the latter to be stowed away under the vehicles to distribute their weight. The Horsa's take-off is activated by a rolling undercarriage discarded after take-off. Basically they were to land on a sledge, but the use of wheels was often favoured, permitting manoeuvring . In 1941, one of the first American Jeeps will be stowed in a Horsa, whereafter cargo specifications will be laid down for all material expected to be hauled or trailed by the plane (trailers, 6 pdr anti-tank and US 75mm

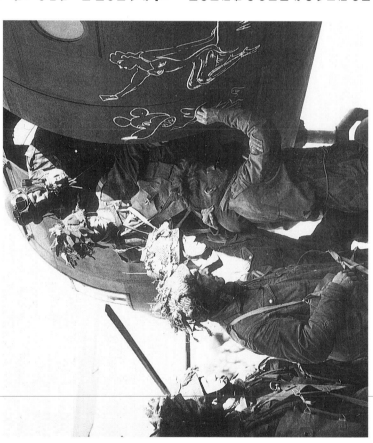

The glider shock absorbing glider helmet designed by the RAF is made of riveted fibre-proof. The leather lower parts the headset indispensable for communications between the glider and and towing plane: a microphone mask type 10A 12572 (snap fastened at left and retained at right by a flat hook) and the earphones all being of the standard RAF pattern. The silk scarf so typical for every British pilot and glider wings are clearly shown.

light howitzers).

By 1944, the glider's tail becomes an independent part, held in place by 8 explosive bolts. This emergency method speeded up the unloading of the plane, especially when its nose became inbedded in a wall or tree.

The Hamilcar

The shortage of transport materiel and lack of an armoured element being the weakness of the airborne troops in 1941, endeavours were undertaken for the construction of a wooden glider plane capable to hold a light tank a 17 pounder anti-tank cannon, the whole being towed by a Stirling or Halifax.

Weighting a total of 14 tons when loaded, the Hamilcar will be a monoplace glider, its wings mounted near on the top of the fuselage. Two external opening doors are installed in its ample dimensionned nose. The lowe-

INSIGNIA OF THE GLIDER PILOT REGIMENT

We note that the regiment belongs to the Army Air Corps of which this officer is wearing the distinctive insignia. Accordingly, his rank pips are embroidered on a Cambridge Blue underlay from april 1942 on (though no arm of service strip of the same colour exits).

Above: worn on the maroon beret, the cap badge carries the cipher of the corps.

Below, the shoulder title worn on the sleeve along with the divisional insignia and airborne strip.
Below: the Army Flying Badge was was available in two versions: embroidered (other ranks') and bullion (officers').
Instruction ACI 768 of 11 April 1942 specified that this insignia was to be issued to light aviation and glider pilots. Sewn on the left side of the chest on both the jacket and the Dension smock, the insignia did not entitle its wearer to any pay increase. Retained by pilots who had left active service, the insignia was awarded to pilots who had successfully completed training with the Elementary Flying Training School, the Glider Training School and the Glider Operational Training Unit. Later on, graduating from the first school became the only prerequisite. The insignia was awarded on advice of the officer commanding the Glider Pilot Regiment until August 1944, and by the officer commanding the Glider Pilot Depot thereafter.

Another insignia for glider co-pilots was defined in Instruction 1128 of 19 August 1944.

Above: This sergeant is a glider pilot commissioned with 1st or 2nd Wing, the Glider Pilot Regiment. This unit delivered the Airlanding Brigade during the Normandy invasion. Adorned with the Army Air Corps insignia, the maroon beret is carried in a smock pocket. Individual armament consists of web belt and pistol holster.

ring of the fuselage toward the ground, facilitating loading and unloading was achieved by adding an hydraulic system to the undercarriage. These could be started shortly before tak-off (the exhaust gasses escaping through a special vent) Retaining straps would be automatically released by pulling a simple string. □

AIRBORNE FORCES EQUIPMENT

The individual equipment used to British paratroopers on operations is displayed at left. All these items are on regular issue. Readers should not that when leaving Britain for Normandy, the paratroopers had left their large packs behind.

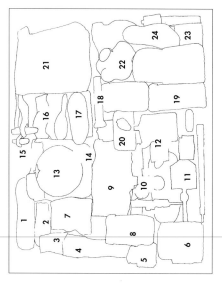

1. - Anti-gas cape made of impregnated cloth. Can also be used a a raincoat or as a sleepling bag as it retains body heat.

2. - Khaki woollen gloves protecting the hands during the drop.

3 - Grey woolknit socks.

4. - Wirecutters in their web carrier. Secured to the belt.

5 - Mark III prismatic compass in its felt-lined carrier. Secured to the belt.

6. - Binoculars in waterproof web case, slung around the neck or secured to the belt.

7. - Ration bag on which a packet of biscuits and a portable heater are displayed.

8. - Basic pouches and 1967 Pattern webbing as issued to infantry. With spike bayonet, entrenching tool (the carrier of which contains a dubbin box and shoe rags), water bottle and set of straps.

9. - Holdall containing from left to right: a cardboard button-board, a brass polish box, a soap box, a tooth brush, a shaving stick in its bakelite box, a pair of shoelaces, a bakelite razor (a metal razor is also shown), razor blades, three types of eating utensils and one metal mirror in its cardboard carrier placed on a towel.

10. - Tin holding a bar of Blanco.

11 - Steel part of the entrenching tool. The handle is fitted with a bayonet lug.

12. - Enamelled mug.

13. - Maroon beret with Parachute Regiment Badge.

14. - Haversack with messtin and box containing chocolate or sweets.

15. - Toggle rope (with large and small strands).

16. - Undershirt and underpants, with brush and hairbrush.

17. - Plimsolls, made of cloth with rubber soles.

18. - Flashlight with coloured lenses.

19. - Mk III Basic Pouch large than the Mark II so as to accommodate Sten magazines.

20. - Brown and green face veil, and torch.

21. - Large pack. Too cumbersome in action, it was only used by support and service units to carry special equipment.

22. - Light gasmask in waterproof web container, lens cleaning fluid and protective ointment.

23. - Anti-gas eyeshields with spare lenses.

24. - Studded combat boots and foot powder.

RATIONS AND SMALL EQUIPMENT

1 - 24 hours rations set containing one beef tin (a), one dehydrated soup bag, three bars of chocolate with added vitamins, tea and powdered milk (b), powdered lemon drink (c), sugar, salt, porridge (d) and biscuits (e).

2. - Oxocubes.

3 - Sealed emergency ration. Only opened on orders, it contains chocolate with added vitamins.

4. - Self-heating soup tin. Heated by lighting the candle placed in the middle opening of the tin.

5. - Water purifying tablets.

6. - Folding stove with solid fuel tablets.

7. - Oil lamp.

8. - Biscuits.

9. - Clasp knife.

10. - Survival kit as issued to RAF crews. Some paratroopers are known to have used some of these. Fitted with a transparent lid and fitting snugly inside the pocket thanks to their curved shape, these kits contained malt tablets and tinned milk, sweets with added vitamins, matches, chewing gum, compass, thread and needles, razor and soap, water purifying tablets, an iodine bottle and a plastic bag to use as a water container.

11. - Morphine syringe in plastic wrapper.

12. - Torch.

13. - Paybook and ID tags, British currency.

14.- Infantry training manual.

15. - Vaseline.

16. - Anti-mosquito cream.

17. - Foot powder.

18. - Playcards.

19. - Matches and cigarettes.

20. - Field dressings.

21. - Dibbin.

22. - Bugle (used to rally the paratroopers after the drop).

23. - Sewing kit.

24. - Vacuum flask.

25. - Small folder (often carried by airborne soldiers).

26. - Pad and letter-cards.

27. - Regulation issue whistle with leather tab.

28. - Folder and ordnance map indicating the main drop zones.

Right. A cross sample of British rations and victuals displayed on Royal Army Ordnance Corps trestles somewhere in Normandy. The set includes chocolate, tea, sausages, beans, steak and kidney pudding and a large tin of biscuits *(IWM)*

THE COLLAPSIBLE TROLLEY was used to carry equipment and served as a substitute for light vehicles. Available in limited numbers, it was folded up before being loaded into the transport aircraft where it was secured to a special rack. The trolley consists of a steel frame fitted with two wheels, and of a canvas tray to carry the load. The trolley can be assembled in a short time by inserting the cross-struts and tightening the large knurled knobs fitted on the frame. No tools are needed for this operation. The trolley is steered like a wheelbarrow and towed by three men.

Above right:

THE AIR DROPPABLE WICKER BASKET (pannier) had no reinforcements and was mostly used to carry clothing, rations or medical supplies. It had a canvas handle at each corner for carrying. The pannier was dropped with a standard container parachute. The

Folding Bicycle). Light and practical, the folding bicycle came in handy for troops devoid of motor transport. The bicycle could be airdropped on its own or carried by the paratrooper in the same way as the leg bag, issued to dispatch riders, the bicycle sometimes replaced motorbikes. The frame of the model shown here, a BSA, was hinged at the middle and was fastened by two screws. The plain pedals fitted in the pedal and gear mechanism and were secured by spring loaded keys. The wheel are positioned on top of each other and secured together with straps. The pedals folded inward so as to be kept out of the way during transport. Ae rifle or a bag could be carried on the frame.

VEHICLES ALLOTTED TO THE AIRBORNE BRIGADE

- Mk. V bicycles — 1907
- Folding motorbikes — 1362
- 125cc motorcycles — 529
- 350cc motorbikes — 704
- Jeeps — 904
- Light cars — 141
- Bren carriers — 25
- Ambulances — 24
- 750kg trucks — 129
- Three-tone trucks — 438
- Prime movers — 26
- Trailers — 935
- Collapsible trolleys — 21

Airborne equipment displayed by the ROAC in early 1943. From left to right: oversmock, pannier, trousers, helmet and collapsible bicycle. On the floor are a parachute rack, a Sten ammunition magazine, a container parachute, a Bren valise and canvas jerkins. Right: an SMLE valise, and a leg valise for the Sten MkV which, like the Welbike folding motorbike (centre), was not used on 6 June 1944. (IWM)

Left:
An F-type container for N°21 radio set. The set could be dissembled and placed into partitions where it was secured by thick felt pads. The shock absorbing device is clearly visible.

Bottom left: Type E container for N°18 radio set. (IWM).

Below:
Homing pigeons were indispensable auxiliaries to Royal Corps Signallers. The birds were carried in containers secured to the parachute harness. The fast release mechanism was the same as that fitted to the leg bag. When the picture was taken in 1942, British paratroopers were still issued with Sten mark III submachine-guns. For easier transport, the stock was dissassembled and secured alongside the weapon by its sling, and the assembly was slipped into the harness. This method was also suitable for the Sten Mark V types used in June 1944. (IWM).

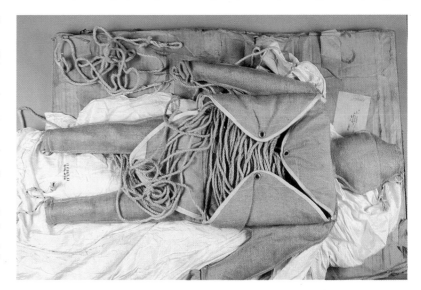

Above: Airborne dummies such as the one displayed above were used to lure the Germans away from the drop zones during the night preceding the landings. Found in its original crate, this exceptional piece carries the manufatuer's label and was stamped by the RAF which dropped it later over Normandy. The padded 'body' is made of coarse canvas, and has the parachute bag fastened to its 'stomach'. The static line can be seen in the right foreground. The canopy was made of white cotton or silk (as here) to be more conspicuous in the darkness.

Below: Transmitters have set up a radio set and installed telegraphic lines in the outpost they have hastily built behind the front lines. In the foreground, a dispatch rider is readying his folding bicycle.

The mortar rounds secured to the bicycle rack will be taken to the front line where they are badly needed. To the left are a container and its parachute and in the background, a black parachute is hanging from a tree.

Above left: Invasion currency and right, the famous N°82 grenade invented in 1941 by Colonel Gammon of 1st Airborne Battalion. Centre: the Fairbairn Sykes dagger was issued to all British airborne forces involved in the June 1944 Invasion. The model shown here has a knurled handle, the type the most frequently encountered during the June 1944 operation.

Below:
Supply containers developed from the RAF 'bombcell'. The infantry versions have the CLE markings (Central Landing Establishment). In the background is a version to drop arms, machine gun, mortars, and mortar rounds. The racks which hold container in the bomb bay are secured by two metal strips. In the foreground: a type H container, its interior divided into partitions each identified by a label describing its content (explosives and armament). The container is reinforced by a rod. Its parachute container is located on the left to be opened by the static line.

Centre: a pouch holding the RAF's escape kit, containing a silk map of France indicating escape routes to the neighbouring countries. It also holds a minute compass with magnetic button. Sewn on the battle dress shoulder strap the button had a luminous dot.

INDIVIDUAL AND HEAVY ARMAMENT

Right inset: This airborne fusilier is armed with the PIAT, a fearsome anti-tank weapon when used over short distances. its has been cocked and a projectile lies in the barrel, ready to be fired. its maximum useful range against armour is 100 meters.

hand fire. It will mostly fire smoke grenades.

INDIVIDUAL WEAPONS

1 - Dust cover for rifle and machine-gun.

2 - 'Valise' protecting the SMLE during the descent, made of thick felt, it is strapped to the body in the same fashion as the leg bag, and was released shortly before touchdown, dangling from a long white strap.

3 - Basic pouch with lightweight bandoleer holding rifle clips, protected by cardboard boxes. 100 rounds are carried by each man, in addition to a Bren magazine.

4 - Instructions manual describing Allied and enemy armament.

5 - Lee-Enfield N°4 Mark III(T) sniper rifle with N°432 Mark I telescope fitted.

6 - Bayonet N°4 Mark V for SMLE and Sten Mark V

7 - SMLE N°4 Mark I *

8 - MP Sten Mark II (S) with pistol grip, a version of the Sten Mark II with silencer. 'S'means 'special purpose', the silencer is covered by a canvas shroud, and the recoil, spring is modified. This design will be issued to the Pathfinders. Above 32-round standard Sten magazine.

9 - Sten Mark V. A special version for airborne use with two pistol grips and bayonet lug. More than 350 000 Mark V Stens had been assembled in government plants before 6 June,1944. It equips officers and NCO's, machine gunners and motor crews. Posed in front of the gun's pistol grip is a box of 9mm ammunition.

10 - Extra magazine belt capable of holding seven Sten magazines.

11 - Sten magazine loader.

12 - Special bayonet frog with pouch holding the Sten's magazine loader.

13 - 9mm ammunitions boxes, at left, a lot manufactured by Winchester.

14 - 1911 automatic pistol.

15 - magazine pouch for 1911 auto pistol and Browning HP.

16 - 45 US ammunition box.

17 - Browning HP 9mm pistol made by Inglis in Canada. It's distribution was not completed in june, 1944.

18 - Enfield N°2 Mark I* Cal 38 revolver with pattern 37 holster which incorporated a cleaning rod.

19 - Three Fairbairn-Sykes daggers with fluted handles, these being the most commonly used type in june 1944. At left, a copper, plated version, at the centre, a nickel plated and at right a bronze plated one. The tip of the leather sheath is fitted with a metal reinforcement , the leather tabs stitched in the sheath are meant to be sewn on the trousers, though sometimes they were also buttoned. This-2 inch mortar crew supports the advance of a combat group. Handy and a lightweight, this mortar, shortened for airborne use will often be used without its elevating device for ioff-

HEAVY WEAPONS

1 - Bren Mark I machine-gun, with apperture sight and telescope bipod.

2 - Maintenance bag for loader/second Bren gunner, holding: the spare barrel, cleaning rod, cold weather type lubricant, graphite grease, rags and cleaning swabs, the gas cylinder cleaning tool, and model 'S' dust cover.

3 - Maintenance kit for Bren gunner: disassembling tool, pull-through cleaning kit, oil flask, box with spare parts.

4 - Box of .303 cartridges.

5 - PIAT (Projector, Infantry, Anti-Tank) 115,000 were manufactured, production started in 1942.

6 - PIAT projectiles.

7 - Device enabling the PIAT to fire mortar rounds. It is placed in the barrel of the weapon so as to fire 2-inch mortar grenades.

8 - Cardboard transportation cylinders for three PIAT rounds.

9 - 2-inch mortar, the infantry's light support weapon, shortened for airborne use and mostly employed with smoke grenades.

10 - Elevating device for 2 inch mortar, often discarded to allow off-hand firing.

11 - Upper : flare grenade with parachute; lower : smoke grenade and explosive grenade.

13 - Cardboard cylinders to carry 6sixmortar rounds.

14 - Aldis signalling lamp, with morse code lever.

A - Hawkins anti-tank mine, detonating under the weight of a tank.

B - 'Clam' magnetic mine used against all vehicles.

C - Smoke grenade.

D - Pressure detonator.

E - Set of plyers to tighten igniters.

F - N°82 plastic-charge grenade.

G - Mills N°36 defensive grenade.

H - N°69 plastic charge fragmentation grenade.

I - N°73 incendiary grenade.

J - Primary explosives sticks.

K - Primary explosive cone.

M - Delay igniting fuses.

L - Plastic explosive and '808', also available roll-shapped.

M - Delay igniting fuse.

N - Box with detonators.

O - Bickford fuse and cigarettesand cigarettes for lightning.

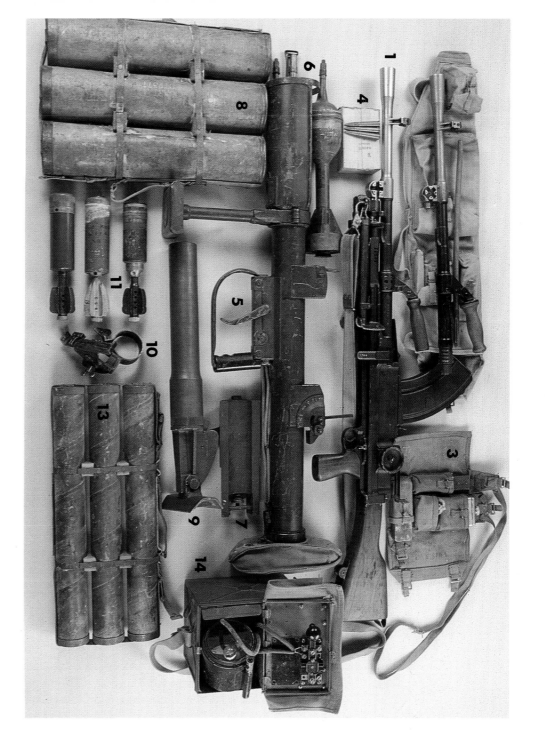

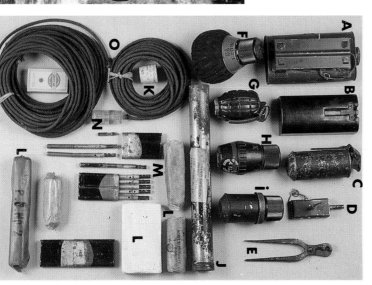

AIRBORNE INSIGNIA

A complete set of insignia AS worn by the 6th Division is displayed on the opposite page. Other ranks and NCOs wore rank Army insignia (see Militaria 46), while ranks of the army air corps (Glider Pilot Regiment and Parachute Regiment) were embroidered on dark blue underlaying known as 'Cambridge blue'.

Cap Badge

All divisional personnel wore the universal maroon beret, adorned with the regimental insignia, corps or service. This was also adopted by its officers who ceased to wear the picked cap, even with the service dress. the famous beret the British Paratroops was to earn them the the nickname of 'Red Devils'.

The Shoulder Tabs

The colour of background and lettering of the insignia covered in this study are regulated by the N° 905 directive of 12 June 1943, which specified (among other things) the type of the lettering to be used. The various units which made up the 6th Airborne, established in early May 1943, will be issued with regulation shoulder tabs, with the exception made of existing units and officers transferred to the new division. This explains why non-regulation insignia are seen on contemporary photographs, this practice resulting from persisting regimental traditions.

The Formation Sign

The insignia of the 6th Airborne, as well as those of the others divisions, have been selected by their Staff and presented to the War Office for approval. Each man will receive two pairs of insignia, one to be sewn on the sleeves of the battledress, the other pair reserved for the Service and Walking-out dress . The officers will also wear theirs on the service dress jackets but then only when on home duty. The insignia are available in right and left versions, the Bellerophon's lance always pointing to the front. Two main types are issued: the regulation model, printed on cotton, distributed by the Ordonance Corps, and the privately purchased ones, the former being the most common while the latter were preferred by officers. The famous Pegasus, the brain-

Top left: A perfectly dressed parachute infantryman. This private of the parachute regiment wears the reglementary set of insignia on his blouse sleeve, made to official specifications. All are issue-type patches, printed on cotton, including the parachute wings

child of artist Edward Seago, who was at that time the officer in charge of the camouflage at the Southern Command. It will be approved in May 1942. Its colours, maroon and light blue were those worn by Brigadier Browning while participating in horse races.

Set on a maroon background, the design was inspired by Greek mythology. It represents 'Bellerophon', a legendary hero, riding a winged-horse, Pegasus, while engaging a fire-breathing monster. The Pegasus underwent its batism of fire in North Africa in November 1942 and will subsequently be worn by the 1st Airborne Division raised during the winter of 1942-43. On 14 May, 1943, during a meeting with General Page, Chief of the Army General Staff in Great Britain, General Gale suggested that the insignia be awarded to the 6th Airborne. On this occasion, General Gale said that no new insignia was needed, but expressed the wish that the Pegasus should be worn by all airborne units to show that they belonged to one large familly.

Furthermore, the 'esprit de corps' would be maintained by men transferred from one unit to another. General Browning readily agreed, because he too wished to have all airborne units operating under one and same insignia. Thus, Pegasus became the universal symbol of all British airborne forces, irrespective of unit or function. It is still being worn today.

The Parachute Qualification Badge

Approved on 28 September 1940, (Army Council Instruction 1589) this skill-at-arms badge will be awarded to the men who have been trained at Ringway Base by RAF instructors. Worn by all members of the parachute units, even by those later assigned to other army branches, the qualification will never entitle the wearer to any pay increase. In addition to standard drill, training will consist of three preliminiary jumps from the gondola of a balloon from an altitude of 300 meters, followed by four jumps from a plane, completed by a night drop, and culminating in a field excise.

The 'wings' can only be taken away from paratroopers who have refused to jump, or who have failed to show up for a pre-jump inspection. 'Wings' cannot be forfeited for any other reason.

Left: This Oxfordshire and Buckinghamshire Light Infantry member is wearing the traditional distinctive insignia of this unit. On his sleeve we remark the Pegasus and airborne strip, made by two different manufacturers, the regimental insignia and the cap badge pinned on a green circular patch (the light infantry's traditional colour) sewn on the red beret. Note also the sleeve title . On the lower sleeve, the non-regulation patch of the glider infantr is embroidered in light blue thread.

Insignia Of The 6th Airborne Division

1 - Cap badge of the Army Air Corps and variants.
1a - Plastic version.
1b - Embroidered title of the Army Air Corps (Pathfinders of the 22nd Independant Company).
1c - Embroidered title of the Glider Pilot Regiment.
2 - Cap badge of the Parachute Regiment and variants (the insignia's lion and crown are irreverently called 'dog and basket' by the paratroops).
2a - Mode of attaching (ring and pin).
2b - Clasp.
2c - Plastic version.
2d - Service dress button.
2e - Collar insignia.
2f - Printed insignia.
2g - Shoulder lanyard of the 8th Battalion.
3 - Enlisted cap badge for the 1st Canadian Parachute Battalion.
3a - Plastic version.
3b - Embroidered title.
4 - Cap badge and embroidered title of the Devonshire Regiment.
5 - Cap badge and embroidered title of the Oxfordshire and Buckinghamshire Light Infantry superimposed on a green background (the light infantry colour of arms).
6 - Cap badge of the royal ulster rifle.
6a - Larger version. both are fixed on the rifle dark green colour of arms.
6b - Embroidered title.
7 - Cap badge and printed title of the Royal Armoured Corps.
8 - Cap badge and printed title of the Royal Artillery Regiment
9 - Cap badge and printed title of the Royal Engineers.
9a - variant for beret.
10 - Cap badge and printed title of the Royal Corps of Signals.
11 - Cap badge and printed title of the Reconnaissance Corps.
12 - Cap badge and printed title of the Royal Army Chaplains Department.
12a - Cap badge for catholic chaplains.
12b - Cap badge for Jewish chaplains.
13 - Cap badge and printed title of the Royal Army Service Corps.
14 - Cap badge and printed title of the Royal Army Medical Corps
15 - Cap badge and printed title of the Royal Army Ordnance Corps.
16 - Cap badge and printed title of the Royal Electrical and Mechanical Engineers.
17 - Cap badge and printed title of the Corps of Military Police. Centre: placement of patches on the battledress sleeve of Parachute Rgiment staff.

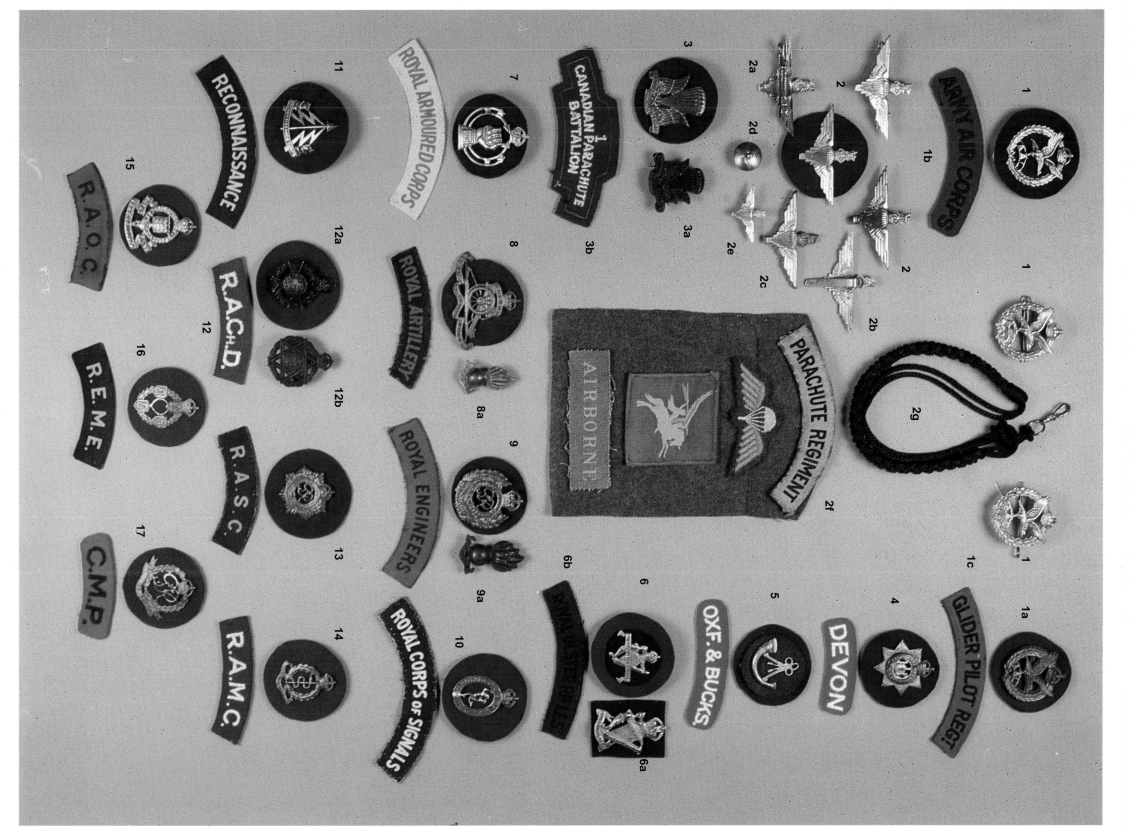

11   RECONNAISSANCE

ROYAL ARMOURED CORPS   7

CANADIAN 1 PARACHUTE BATTALION   3

2a   2   2d   ARMY AIR CORPS   1

1b

3a   3b

2e   2c   2b   1

15   R.A.O.C.

12a

R.A.C.H.D.   12

ROYAL ARTILLERY   8

16   R.E.M.E.

12b

8a

AIRBORNE   PARACHUTE REGIMENT   2f

2g

17   R.A.S.C.

ROYAL ENGINEERS   9

13

1c

9a

C.M.P.

14   R.A.M.C.

ROYAL CORPS OF SIGNALS

10

6b   6

ROYAL ULSTER RIFLES

5   OXF. & BUCKS.

DEVON   4

GLIDER PILOT REGT.   1a

6a

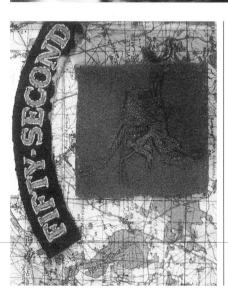

Airborne Insignia

Three sets are issued, two for the battle dress blouse and one for the Denison smock. From 17 June 1942 onwards, it has to be sewn 51 mm from the top of the right sleeve (Instruction 1274 from 17 June 1942, cancelling Instruction 204 from 12 February 1941, which prescribes its position between the elbow and armpit, irrespective of the space needed for the rank insignia). It will not be worn on the overcoat and Denison smock. From 1942 onwards, it will also be worn by all qualified personnel of the airborne division unassigned to any of the parachute infantry brigades.

The Airborne Strip

The men of the airborne forces do not wear the coloured 'arms of service strips' as issued to the services of the army (the shoulder titles being a substitute for these, at least on the blouse). In their stead, a maroon cloth strip is sewn, embroidered on imprinted with light blue airborne lettering. The 'strip, airborne', is introduced by ACI 2816 from 31 October 1942 for all non-parachute qualified airborne personnel, to further distinguish them from the rearward support services of the unit. The strip is sewn on each of the blouse sleeves, beneath the formation sign. Contemporary pictures reveal that the strips were often worn by the paratroopers, (including the Canadians) clearly showing their belonging to the airborne service.

Airborne Qualification Patch for Staff Unassigned to Parachute Units

The instruction ACI 1274 from 17 June, 1942 introduces an insignia representing a white parachute embroi-

dered on on a vertical rectangle made of brown cloth to be awarded to parachute qualified personnel not belonging to a regular parachute unit or not being parachute instructors. Surnamed 'the electric bulb' it is initially sewn on the position prescribed for this particular patch. From October 1942 onward, it was displaced to the right forearm of the battledress blouse, or in case of officer's, on the same spot but on the service dress jacket, and sewn 6 inches (15cm) above the cuff. The warrant officers wear the patch just under their rank markings. Only one pair is given to each man, as it cannot be worn on the overcoat or Denison smock.

The Glider Infantry Qualification Badge

These men, as well as those previously involved in operationnal landings, will wear this patch on the battledress right arm or in the case of officers, on the service dress. It depicts a stylized glider plane embroidered in blue thread on a brown cloth oval. The plane should point to the front. Versions exist with the regimental distinctive colours as background, the same colours being frequently used as a background for the title. Though no trace of authorization can be found, it was seemingly created by the staff of the airborne forces. To conclude this chapter, we should mention the shoulder lanyard and slip over tabs worn by a/b troops on the blouse and sometimes on the smock: 7th Batallion: green, 8th Batallion : dark blue, 9th: red, 12th: light blue, 13rd: black, Royal Ulster Rifles: green, Oxfordshire and Buckinghamshire: blue.

Left: The title worn by Major Howard on 6 June. It retains the original denomination of the 2nd Batalion of the Oxfordshire and Buckinghamshire, 52nd Regiment of Foot. The red thread lettering had a yellow border and was printed on a night blue background. Introduced in 1942-1943, it was retained by the division's veteran personnel. By 1944, the regulation title is the one shown on fig.5, page 51. Below the title, we observe the embroidered Pegasus, both insignia being worn concurrently.

Above: 28 April 1945. After the crossing of the Rhine, Monty awards the Military Cross to Captain RAA Smith of the 2nd Batallion of the Oxfordshire and Buckinghamshire. The officer wears the blue shoulder lanyard and regulation scarlet title with white lettering. The white parachute insignia is sewn on the sleeve. It was worn by qualified paratroopers unassigned to a regular parachute unit. For this event, the Field Marshall has replaced his famous black beret with a maroon model. This beret was presented to him in August 1943, by Major General Hopkinson who first commanded the airborne division.

Left: May 1944, this corporal still wears the qualification patch 51mm from the armpit, the regulation way is displayed on his neighbour's uniform. The trooper has strapped his Mark V Sten to his harness, along with the toggle rope.and has a US M1911 automatic pistol.

Near the end of Agust 1944, General Montgomery takes part in award ceremony for the men of the 6th Airborne. This sergeant of the 1st Batallion of Royal Ulster Rifles wears the regulation cap badge with its traditional dark green (Rifle Green underlay). The slip over on his shoulder tabs sidentify his battalion.

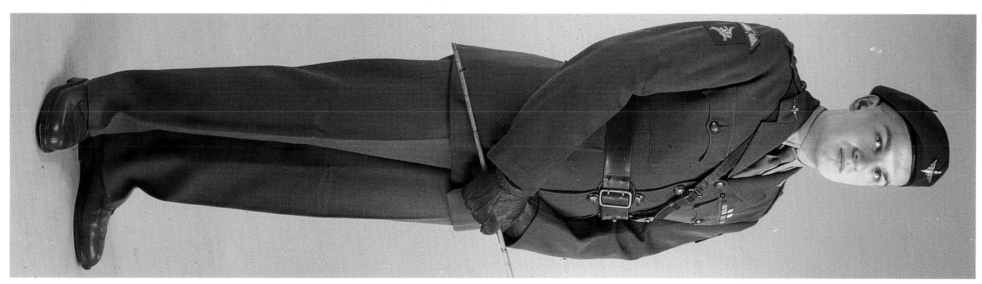

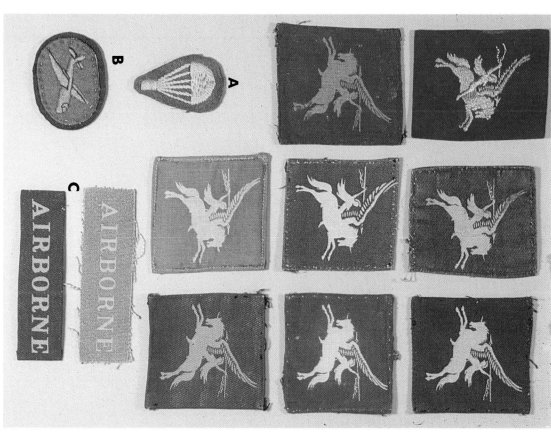

Above: Various versions of the parachute wings (an embroidered version also exists). At lower left: A bullion embroidered officer's model, the wings showing a raised motif.
Center: The Canadian wings, embroidered here on a black background.
Left: This Parachute Regiment lieutant displays his service dress, before attending a ceremony. The jacket is the simplified pattern introduced in 1942, the rank pips are of the regular type. The Sam Browne belt and stick are noteworthy.

Below: The various maker's version of the airborne division Pegasus, the printed one being the most commonly seen.
Upper left: A privately purchased version for officers.
A - Insignia of parachute qualified personnel unassigned to a regular parachute unit.
B - Non-regulation glider infantry patch unit, also sewn on the right forearm.
C - Airborne strips, worn by all operational personnel of the airborne division.

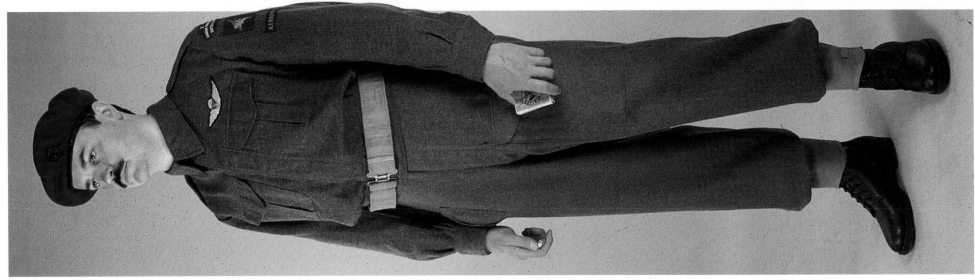

CANADIAN PARATROOPERS

By Bernard Petitjean and Jocelyn Carnier

A MERE few months after the creation of a British airborne corps did the Canadians express their wish to raise an airborne unit. This project was entrusted to Colonel ELM Burns. Although the decision was made in August 1940, the new unit did not come into being until April 1942 when its creation was approved by the House of Commons

In June, Lieutnant Colonel Keeffer went to Fort Benning, the US airborne infantry training centre, to undertake a study of the methods and material employed by the Americans. The outcome of Burns' and Keeffer's findings, and the encouraging results of the Ringway school in Britain, prompted the National Defence Headquarters to raise an independent parachute batallion for for the defence of the Canadian homeland. This decision was approved by the Secretary of Defence on 1 July 1942, and the 1st Canadian Parachute Batallion was placed under the Command of of Lieutnant Colonel Bradbrook.

From Fort Benning to Camp Shilo

The 1st Batallion was organized along the same lines as British units, to include seven staff company and three fusilier companies amounting to a total of 26 officers and 5,910 other ranks. Recruits were provided by the regular army. The Rousseau brothers, for example, left the Chaudiere Regiment to join the new unit, one of them being killed at Normandy during the night of 5 June. Training intensified from August to December 1943. British jump techniques required some adaptation for those having graduated in the USA. The British, for instance used only one parachute, whereas the Americans had two. Also training jumps in America were made from towers while the British used balloons. For combat jumps, the British employed modified bombers with a floor hatch installed the Americans used a C-47 with a side door. A reinforcement and insctruction company was raised numbering ca 400 men. The exercises involved increasingly larger number of men, with manoeuvres being conducted at brigade level followed by manoeuvres at divisional level. Without doubt, the batallion would play an important role in the invasion, which, at this moment was on everybody's mind. On 24 May, the batallion left Bulford for Down Ampney transit Camp where the 'Canucks', as they were nicknamed, eagerly awaited D-Day among their comrades from the 3rd Brigade (8+9th Batallion of the Parachute Regiment) commanded by brigadier James Hill.

Jump Over Normandy

The 6th Division was briefed with occupying the sector between the Orne and La Dives rivers after creating defensives positions. The Canadian Batallion was assigned certain missions : 'A' Company would have to support the advance and attack of the 9th Batalion against the Merville Battery. Some element of 'C' Company wouldreach the bridge over the Divette at Varaville which they would destroy during an RAF bombing. Supported by the men of the 3rd Para Squadron, they would then demolish a fortified area at Varaville, but sustained heavy losses during the afternoon of 6 July. 'B' Company, nearly

Right:
June 1944, 10am, on Hartwell Air Base, Great Britain. This para of 'C' Company, the 1st Canadian Battalion, is getting ready for the mission entrusted to his unit: marking the drop zones. Soon, he will smear his face with black cream before donning the parachute harness and take the equipment to the aircraft. Like many others, the man has felt that it was unnecessary to wear his oversmock over his Denision smock. His inflatable life preserver has been secured, but its straps are worn slack so as not to hamper inflating.

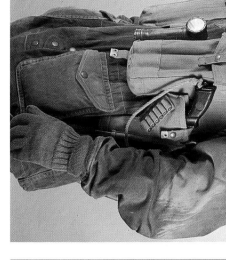

Left:
Photographed in Great Britain during a furlough, this soldier of the 1st Battalion has just received the newly-introduced plastic insignia. The battalion's shoulder title, the 6th Airborne 'Pegasus', and the 'Airborne' strip are regulation issue. The Canadian airborne qualification badge is worn above the left chest pocket. With the exception of its colour, the Canadian battledress was identical to the British 1937 Pattern.

Left:
Like all paratroopers of the 6th Airborne Brigade, the soldier has been issued with a Fairbairn Sykes dagger. The weapon is carried in an American-made M-6 scabbard. Th Mark 1 helmet has a riveted leather chinstrap. The Denison smock is almost new as shown by its bright colours.

Right.
Contemporay photographs show that some items were on specific issue to Canadian paras: in addition to his submachine-gun, the soldier is armed with an Enfield handgun carried in a tank crew-type holster for quicker draw if threatened. The weapon is secured to the shoulder by a web lanyard.
An American TL 122a flashlight is secured to the belt. The hands are protected by regulation issue woollen gloves. A toggle rope and a face veil complete the equipment.

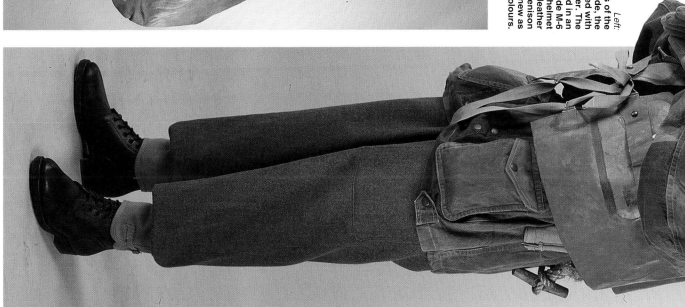

Canadian Paratoopers

anihilated, blew up the Robehomme bridge over the Dives at around 5.30am. It took hold on the hill of Robehomme and remain in the sector until 7 June, when it arrived at Le Mesnil. From 'A' company, severly scattered, only some 30 men managed to remain together, joined by strayed personnel from 6th Airborne units. They joined the 9th Batallion at around 6.30am after the latter's exploit at the Merville batteries, and protection the withdrawal of the survivors as far as Le Plein. 8 June heavy combats occured at Le Mesnil crossroad, where the Germans tried to breach the lines of the 3rd Brigade. On the 10th, they occupied the village of Bréville between the positions of the Canadian Batallion and the 9th British Batallion. The enemy was be chased with the support of 'C' company and left the zone on the 14th. The 17th, the complete brigade is granted a rest and moved to Ouistreham. The Canadian Batallion returns to the Mesnil crossroad on 25 June, when it became involved in position warfare until early July when the complete brigade returned to the rear. On 21 July, strengthened by some hundred men of the instruction company, the Canadians were posted to the edge of the woods of Bavent and Troarn. The offensive started again on 17 August, and the Bavent wood was captured. The 18th, four canal bridges were taken, while the Les Landes bridge remained intact. On the 23 June, Lieutnant Colonel Bradbook leaves the temporary command of the battalion to Major G. A. Eady. On 7 September, the 1st Canadian Batallion return to Britain with the bulk of the division. From the 443 men of the Canadian Batallion who dropped over Normandy, 235 casualties were recorded. Its companies lost 357 men, 83 of whom were killed in combat, 187 wounded and another 87 taken prisoner.

The Ardennes and Varsity

By mid-September, Lt Colonel Niklin took over the batallion's command. Due to the German offensive in the ardennes, the unit was hastily moved to the front on 20 December. It took part in the action with the 6th Airborne from 2 January, until 18 January, 1945, to return to Britain in

1. Where a monument is erected to commemorate the participation of the Canadians to the combats.

wed that there was a larger number of beach obstacles in Normandy than had been encountered on previous landings. A small Navy Combat Demolition Unit was detailed to investigate what might be needed to break through this part of Hitler's Atlantic wall. They rapidly came to the conclusion that the NBB hydrographic sections, who had been trained in demolitions, would not be able to clear sufficient lanes for landing craft. Their report was ignored until it was brought to the top by Cmdr. Carusi of the 6th NBB, which caused two Naval Combat Demolition Units (NCDU) to be attached to each Beach Company for the Normandy landings.

The NCDU were originally composed of 5 navy men (1 officer, 4 ratings), but as information on beach obstacles grew, another 5 demo men from the army were added to each team. Officers were in short supply, so in many cases there was only one navy officer per two units. Shortly before the landings, an additional three navy sailors, detailed as a small boat crew for the rubber raft used to carry supplies, brought the total number of men in the demo units to 13.

The job of the NCDUs was to blow gaps in the obstacles for landing craft. In order not to call attention to their work they planned to set all their charges, then blow the entire gap in one explosion. One of teams developed an explosive charge of C-2 (a plastic explosive) in a tubular canvas bag that had a hook on one end, and a loop on the other. This could be quickly attached to the beam of a 'Belgium gate' obstacle, and when properly placed would collapse the gate inward with no flying debris. These C-2 packs were called 'Hagensen packs' after the inventor, and became standard Navy issue. Purple smoke canisters were carried to warn incoming landing craft that demolitions were about to be set off.

The navy teams worked on obstacles from the sea in, while a separate Army engineer team of 26 men, 2 tanks, and one bulldozer or tankdozer were to work from the beach out. Each group of navy and army

Right: Front of Helmet worn by Joe Geary of platoon A-2, 6th NBB on Omaha Beach. The chin strap was cut by shrapnel on the beach, which also ripped off his helmet net. Each helmet and liner in the unit was hand painted by the owner. The Red arc was worn only by members of the 6th and 7th NBB on Omaha beach.

Below right: Rear view of Joe Geary Helmet. The 'USN' appears to have been worn only by members of A Co. in the 6th NBB.

Below: Original helmet from the 7th NBB. A red arc can be seen above the 'USN', and a grey band has been added around the bottom. It appears that the red arc was worn only by NBB personnel on Omaha Beach, and the gray band was used by all navy units in the Normandy Invasion. (Dave Powers collection)

NAVAL BEACH BATTALIONS HELMET MARKINGS IN NORMANDY

FRONT / BACK

6th NBB A Company — 6th NBB A Company (USN)

6th NBB B Company — 6th NBB B Company

6th NBB C Company — 7th NBB — 6th NBB C Company (TAYLOR)

2nd NBB Medical Section (USN) — 2nd NBB (USN)

8th NBB (Southern France)

teams was called a 'Gap Assault Team', and was to clear an opening in the obstacles 50 yards wide by 300 yards long. Each assault team was to land in an LCT(A) right behind the initial wave of infantry. There was a planned 20 minute period after the gap assault teams landed so they would be able to do their work without having incoming troops interfere with the operation.

The crews of the landing craft were unable to follow the tightly scheduled plan, and most of the demo teams found themselves trying to blow up obstacles which were providing shelter for the infantry. Of the 16 gaps that were to be opened on Omaha beach, the initial confusion meant that only 5 were finished on the morning of 6 June (of which only 1 could be properly marked). By evening this had been raised to 13 gaps, and a few days later the entire beach had been cleared of all obstacles.

NCDU Uniforms

There were no American underwater demolition teams in Normandy. At this time the U.S. Navy had only these overstrength NCDUs that were trained to work in the surf. When the tide rose above the obstacles they were forced to stop work until it went down again. In the Invasion they wore gas impregnated HBT coveralls, carried carbines, carried yellow primacord on communications reels (or wrapped it around their helmets), and carried their detonators in condoms. Many of the navy men wore M-2 deck jackets for

Below:
Platoon A-2, 2nd NBB, medical section. This mixture of signalmen and medics shows various methods of painting the helmet. The 2nd NBB was a veteran unit with service in the Mediterranean, so that may account for their being able to obtain tanker's jackets, and the different varieties of painted helmets. The paratrooper boots are quite visible in this shot. (US Navy 80-G-252749)

TABLE OF ORGANIZATION FOR COMPANY B/ 6th NAVAL BEACH BATTALION, JUNE 1944

Company Commander-Lieutenant (Junior grade) E.V. Hall
Communications Officer-Ensign W.D. Ludwig

Company Staff
1 quartermaster
1 radioman
1 signalman
4 seamen

Mess section
8 cooks
2 bakers
9 steward's mates

Demolitions officer
Lieutenant (junior grade) W. Cooper

Navy Combat Demolition Team 22
6 Navy demolition men
5 Army demolition men
3 man Navy small boat crew

Navy Combat Demolition Team 23
6 Navy demolition men
5 Army demolition men
3 man Navy small boat crew

Platoon B - 4
Lieutenant (junior grade) Weathers (Beachmaster) + assistant Beachmaster (officer)

Platoon B - 5
Ensign A.L. Hagerty + assistant Beachmaster (officer)

Platoon B - 6
Lieutenant (junior grade) G. Wade + assistant Beachmaster (officer)

Medical Section
1 doctor (officer)
5 pharmacist mates
3 hospital apprentices

Boat Repair Section
2 carpenter's mates
4 machinist's mates
1 electrician
1 shipfitter

Hydrographic Section
3 petty officers
16 seamen

Communications Section
5 radiomen
3 signalmen

U.S. Naval Beach Battalions

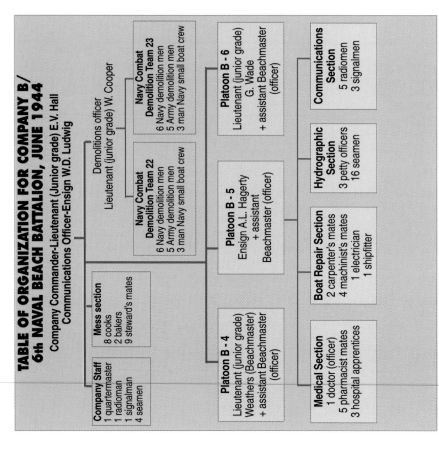

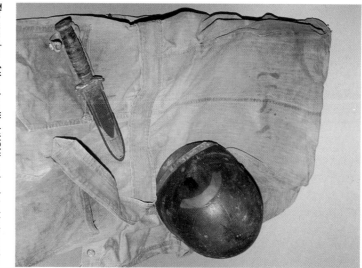

The remains of the stencilled 'USN', and painted belt can be seen on this HBT coveralls which was carried onto Omaha Beach in the pack of Joe Geary of platoon A-2, 6th NBB. He landed in the morning of D-day, and was wounded by mortar fire while sheltering behind a broached landing craft. After making his way to the shore, he returned under fire to the craft to carry a seriously wounded man to safety. He was evacuated from the beach the following morning. After recovering from numerous shrapnel wounds, he served the remainder of the war in the Pacific as part of an APA shore party. The painted belt is only known to have been done in A Co, 6th NBB.

warmth in the surf. Most of them carried 40 pounds of explosives ashore, either TNT or the putty-like C-2. Like the other assault troops, they carried the amphibious gas mask, and first aid kit with morphine syrette.

Carrying explosives in an amphibious landing is a hazardous mission. The navy demo teams suffered 52% casualties on Omaha Beach (dead and wounded). The survivors returned to the States shortly after the invasion, and were used to train men for the Pacific. There were seven Navy Crosses awarded to NCDU men in Normandy, along with many Silver and Bronze Stars. Two of the only three Navy Presidential Unit Citations for Normandy were awards made to the demo units of both Omaha and Utah Beach.

The NCDU on Utah beach had an easier time of it, as the fighting passed swiftly over their beach. One NDCU man located, and captured, 15 Germans who had holed up in a presumed empty bunker. After the landings the Utah beach teams were transferred to the Mediterranean to take part in the Southern France landings. There they attempted to use some experimental radio controlled, explosive landing craft to try and break through beach obstacles. The experimental craft did not perform well, and most of the obstacles had to be blown by hand. The NCDU of Utah beach were the only naval units in Normandy to be awarded the US Navy Unit Commendation Medal.

The lessons learned in Normandy meant that obstacle demolition in the Pacific would be done before the actual invasion, while the water was over the obstacles, not at low tide while the infantry was trying to land. The Pacific Campaign led to many developments in underwater demolition, and eventually to the Underwater demolition teams that still exist today.

Another unknown navy unit were the 'Scouts and Raiders' who had the job of guiding in the first assault waves. They manned the control boats that marked the sea lanes leading to the landing areas. Their boats

A Pharmacists mate (medic) of the 2nd NBB on Utah beach. He wears rain gear and medics pouches, as well as a red cross marked helmet. Photographic evidence of the NBB medical units on Normandy show few red cross arm bands and painted helmets. This is probably due to a fear of snipers, as the equipment list for medics prescribed the armband.

Below.
This remarkable sequence of casualty evacuation from Utah beach shows some of the work of the medical and hydrographic sections of the 2nd NBB. Visible on two of the helmets are faded medical red crosses. This may have been painted in the Mediterranean, and then scraped off as the medics became more battle hardened. In the background can be seen medical jeeps, bulldozers and the markers for lane number 10: an incoming landing craft would line up the two triangles marked '10', and then he would be sure of being in cleared lane #10 through the obstacles. (US Navy 80-G-252625)

and a few other men were hiding behind. The blast caused him multiple shrapnel wounds, ripped off his helmet net, and cut the chin strap of his helmet. As they all ran for the cover of the dunes, Geary went back though the shelling to carry a badly wounded man out of the surf. He made his way up the beach to an aid station, spent the night in a shallow foxhole, and was evacuated the next morning.

One of the seamen from platoon C-9 6th NBB, Bob Giguere, struggled to shore and found himself separated from his unit. A number of infantrymen from the 16th Inf. (1st Div) were trying to break through the German defenses and kept yelling : *Get off the beach! Get off the beach!* Giguere decided it was better to help someone that seemed to know what they were doing, than to sit by himself on the beach, so he pitched in and soon found

▲ *Above.*
USN Petty Officer rating badges.
1. Machinist 2nd class.
2. Electrician 3rd class.
3. Radioman 2nd class.
4. Storekeeper 2nd class.
5. Yeoman 3rd class.
6. Radioman 3rd class.
7. Carpenter 1st class.
8. Shipfitter 3rd class.

U.S. Naval Beach Battalions on D-Day

also fired the rocket barrages that were supposed to hit the beaches just before the first wave. After the NBBs were ashore, the control boats helped keep order off the beach and rescued a number of men floating in the water (to include a few paratroopers dropped off Utah beach).

NBBs on D-Day

Beach battalion units were to be among the first waves to land on the shore. The strong eastward tide, as well as enemy fire, caused many units to land in the wrong location, or out of sequence. The demolition teams had such a hard time opening up clear sea lanes, that by 0830hrs the 7th NBB sent out an order to temporarily cease all landing on the beach until more lanes were open. In the 6th NBB 1st Division sector things operated slightly more to plan, and troops poured ashore.

Since the NBB's were considered highly important to the landings, they did not come in as complete units. They were split up among a number of ships, and assigned to different landing waves. This ensured that a lucky hit would not knock out an entire beach control section. Many of the Omaha beach units were scattered, but gradually the units found their proper destinations and put the plan into action.

By 1200hrs on 6 June, the first ship to shore communications net was established, and three more were put into place later that day. Slowly the fighting moved inland, the shelling of the area slowed down, and the NBB's were able to work unhampered by sniper fire. By 2200 hrs all platoons of the 6th NBB had reorganized and were operating on their assigned beach sectors.

Men of the Invasion

Joe Geary's story is typical. He came in early in the morning of 6 June as member of the hydrographic section, A-2, 6th NBB. He was forced to swim part of the way to the shore, and found cover behind a broached landing craft. The Germans shelled the craft that he

▶ *Above.*
This is landward view of one of the 2nd NBB sites on Utah Beach. Of great interest is the man on the far left. He has both a black and a white lettered 'USN' on his jacket. The day before the landings, an order was sent out to all Navy personnel in the invasion to paint 'USN' in white, 6in. high letters on the front and back of their uniforms. This was to prevent their being mistaken for Germans by the army. This figure is a clear example of someone who had already stencilled USN in black, but then added the larger, white letters.

himself crawling under barbed wire to get at some pill-boxes. The infantrymen tossed him grenades across an anti-tank ditch, and he relayed them to an infantry-man who was able to throw them right into the pillbox opening. He moved up to Colleville-sur-Mer with the infantry, and evacuated a number of Frenchmen hiding in the church shortly before the church steeple was shelled. He took the Frenchmen back to the beach, was wounded by mortar fire, and evacuated the next day. After recovery, he discovered he had been awar-ded the silver star for his actions on the beach. He later was assigned to the marine raiders, and spent a few weeks behind the lines in the Philippines planning for that invasion.

For the first few days the NBB men went about their duties as traffic cops of the beach, bringing in much needed men and equipment. Many of them worked around the clock for the first few days without any sleep. There was always one more landing craft to bring in, or one more batch of wounded to move out. The transfer of supplies from the larger ships to

smaller, and then to the beach was not fast enough to keep the army supplied. In a desperate move the beachmasters tried bringing LSTs right into the shore and letting them dry out on the sand as the tide went down. This allowed vehicles to be driven right off the LST onto dry land, but meant that the ship could unload only once every 14 hours. The DUKWs proved to be worth their weight in gold, as they were able to swim out to the ships, load up and then drive right up to an inland supply dump without having to to be unloaded on the beach. The flat bottomed Rhino Fer-ries enabled other vehicles to be brought into water shallow enough to enable them to drive right onto the beach.

By 12 June the Beach masters had the total tonna-ge of Omaha and Utah beach up to 9,452 tons per day; far above what had been expected. On 15 June the engineers and Seabees completed the artificial 'mulberry harbor' that allowed LSTs to dock and unload without waiting for the tide. This meant that an LST could unload, return to England, load up again

Right.
USN Petty Officer Rating Badges (cont.)
9. Signalman 2nd class.
10. Coxswain (Chief Boatswain's mate) in bullion.
11. Electrician 3rd class.
12. Aviation Ordnanceman 3rd class(a common rating in the NCDUs).
13. Radioman 1st Class
14. Engineer Special Brigades pocket patch (not worn by NBB, as no place on uniform....).
15. Army Amphibious Forces.
16. Navy Amphibious Forces (authorized on 15 June 1944)
17. Early Amphibious forces.
18. Navy dress Blue ruptured duck (Honorable discharge badge).
19. Sharpshooter sleeve qualification mark for Winter Dress blues.
20. Expert Rifleman qualification mark for Summer dress whites.

U.S. Naval Beach Battalions, 1942-1944

and be halfway back to France in the same time it had previously taken to only unload. The beachmasters got ready to turn control of the area over to the 11th Port, who were skilled in port and dock operation.

On June 19th, the worst storm in 40 years hit the French coast. Incoming supplies were negligible for the next three days, and a serious supply shortage developed in the Allied armies. The artificial harbor at Omaha was totally ruined, and suddenly the beachmasters found themselves not only back in the business of supplying the army with everything it needed, but trying to get the beaches cleared of wreckage so they could start to bring in the ships. The storm had left the beaches in worse shape than the invasion landings had. The men of the NBB's, alongside the army engineers, cleared the area in record time, and put many damaged boats back to work.

The Army's lifeline

Working with the knowledge that they were the army's lifeline, the amount of tonnage landed went up beyond what had been expected. An average of 20,000 tons a day, much higher than with the artificial harbor, was brought in on the American beaches to the end of June. This amount rose until winter storms forced a closure of the beaches on 19 Nov. 1944. Had it not been for the skilled and dedicated men keeping the supplies flowing over the beachhead, the combat troops would have faced a severe shortage of food, ammunition, and reinforcements.

Of the 42 officers and 368 enlisted men that had gone ashore with the 6th NBB, 4 officers and 18 enlis-

ted men were killed, 12 officers and 55 enlisted men were wounded. Included in this figure is the battalion commander, Cmdr Carusi, who was accidentally wounded by friendly 20mm flak on 10 June while standing on the slope overlooking Omaha beach.

The men of the NBB's remained on the beaches until 28 June, when most of them were transferred back to the States as instructors at the new navy amphibious training base at Oceanside, California. Most of these went on to become members of APA (Navy Attack Transport) crew shore parties in the later Pacific invasions. On 19 August all remaining 104 men of the 6th NBB turned their duties over to a 50 man detachment from the 5th NBB, and returned to the States.

The 6th NBB was awarded the French Croix de Guerre with palm for its service on Omaha Beach. As the unit was attached to the 5th ESB at the time, all paperwork went through army channels and to this day many of the men have never received the award notification.

Although no other units were as important to the campaign as the combat troops, the NBB's with their beachmasters played a critical role not only in the initial landings in France, but in keeping men and material moving swiftly across the beaches. Had it not been for their expertise, the wreckage of the Mulberry harbor might have spelled doom for the Allied armies. These shore based sailors have never received the recognition they deserve, and it is hoped that with renewed interest and further research more information on them will come to light.

Not only did the NBB's handle evacuation of casualties, but as can be seen in this photo of a 2nd NBB man at Utah Beach, they were involved with getting prisoners off the beaches. The lead guard carries the 1903 Springfield (any Springfield in use by the army at this time would have been the modified 1903A3), and the rear guard carries a carbine. (US Navy 80-G-320898)

The author and editor wish to thank the men of the 6th Naval Beach Battalion who have graciously shared their information and experiences : Joe Geary, Bob Giguere, Joe Vaghi, Dr Lee Parker, Vince Cordack, and Albert Hall as well as Cliff Legerton of the 8th NBB.

One of the communications sections of the 2nd NBB on Utah Beach. Everyone seems to be wearing the foul weather clothing, except for the navy Lt., who wears the foul weather jacket. The helmets of this section have the gray band, with a stencilled 'USN' at the front. Note the use of not just a blinker light and walki-talki, but of the loudspeaker system to verbally direct incoming boats. Note the buckles on the jacket of the man at far left, they are only found on the army style wet weather gear. (US Navy 80-G-252739)

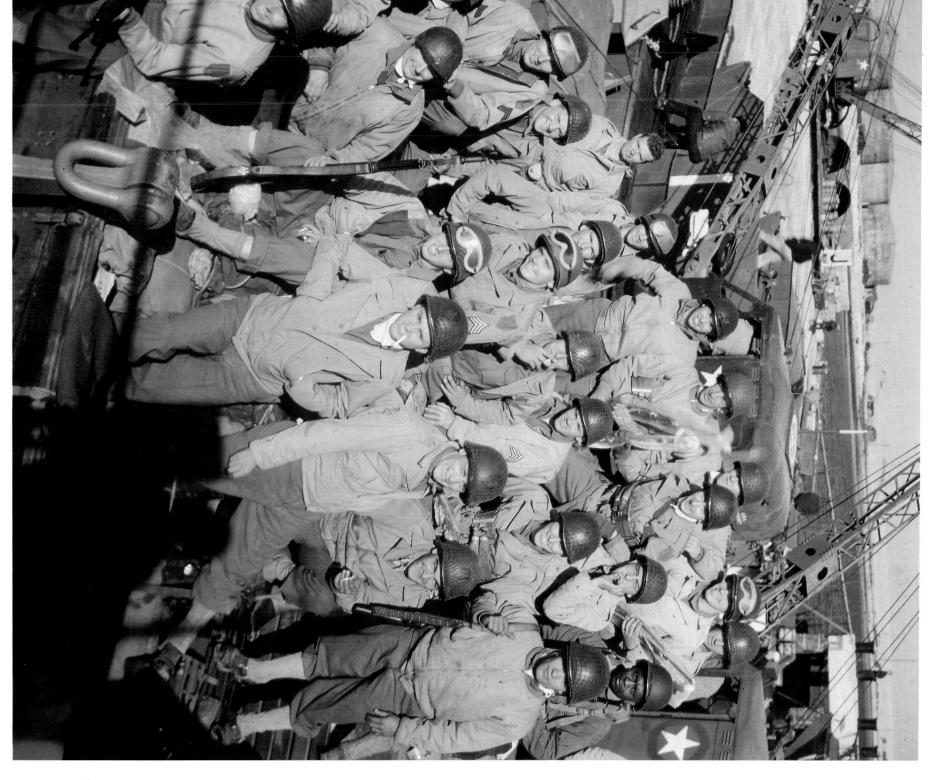

6 JUNE 1944: THE GI OF D-DAY

By Philippe Charbonnier

5 June 1944: along with 1.5 million other GIs who have been arriving in Great Britain since 1942, Private Lawrence is champing at the bit. Like his comrades, Lawrence only has one thought on his mind: the invasion of occupied Europe. Confined in the stifling hold of a transport ship, Lawrence writes his will for the umpteenth time before cleaning his rifle like a competition weapon. Gradually, his confidence is building up again.

Until that fateful morning, Lawrence has had more than his share of ups and downs: the sea sickness which has upset his stomach since boarding the ship; the training in Devonshire; bouts of homesickness, and the tepid beer of British smoke-filled pubs. But there is no reason why he shouldn't survive the war's major amphibious operation. 'Ike' has got everything planned. More than 17,000 men will land with the first wave. The operation can't fail.

But whatever his self-assurance, the 'Dogface's' chances of getting through unscathed are rather thin: this Virginian belongs to the US 29th Infantry Division (attached to the 1st Infantry Division from 17 May to 7 June 1944). The unit's three objectives are the 'Charlie', 'Dog' and 'Easy' sectors stretching between Vierville-sur-Mer and Saint-Laurent, better known now under their codename: 'Omaha'. On 'Bloody Omaha', the division will lose many men, drowned or cut to pieces by the withering fire of the German 352nd Infantry Division, recently created with fresh troops around a cadre of battle-hardened Eastern Front veterans.

The man depicted in this article conveys the typical appearance of a GI about to set foot on French soil.

Uniforms

The amphibious operation had been scheduled for 1 May 1944 and so the Allies had decided to prepare their men's uniforms for the springtime weather. The most noticeable addition to the assault troops' fighting gear was the issue of anti-gas equip-

The 1928 Pattern haversack was carried without its bottom part (the 'pack carrier') for the assault. The pouch on the haversack's flap holds the 'meat can' and the spoon. The 1910 Pattern entrenching tool in its canvas cover is hooked under this pouch. The tool handle is kept firmly in place by one of the haversack closure straps. Among other things, the haversack contained the folded raincoat, spare socks, a towel, the grooming kit and three K-Rations.

The M-1923 cartridge belt had 10 pockets fitted with a pressure stud, each held a Garand rifle clip. The upper row of eyelets was used to secure the haversack straps; the bottom row was meant to hook pieces of equipment (field dressing pocket, bayonet scabbard and canteen).

M-1926 US Navy lifebelt. Loose fitting for quicker inflating, it was sometimes suspended from the shoulders with strings. The tubes for inflating with the mouth are visible on the back. The belt was adjusted to the wearer's waist by a large hook and eye arrangement at the front.

1 —
2
3
4
5

110

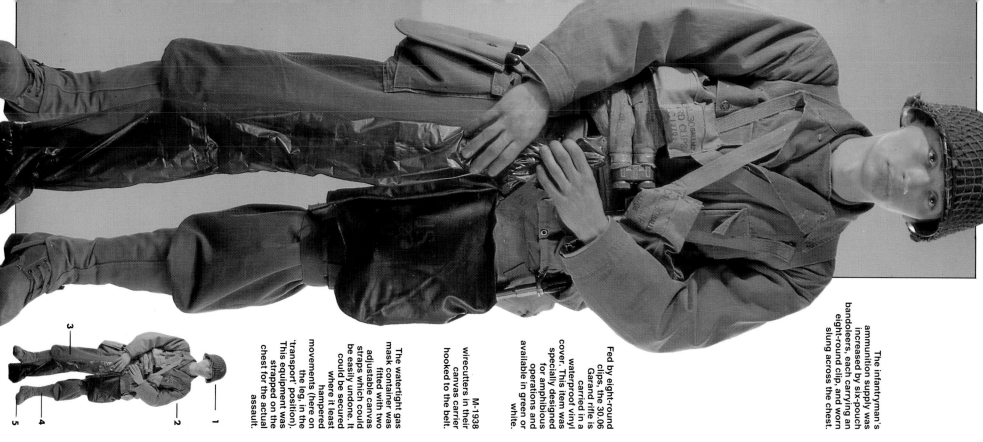

The infantryman's ammunition supply was increased by six-pouch bandoleers, each carrying an eight-round clip, and worn slung across the chest.

Fed by eight-round clips, the 30.06 Garand rifle is carried in a waterproof vinyl cover. This item was specially designed for amphibious operations and available in green or white.

M-1938 wirecutters in their canvas carrier hooked to the belt.

The watertight gas mask container was fitted with two adjustable canvas straps which could be easily undone. It could be secured where it least hampered movements (here on the leg, in the 'transport' position). This equipment was strapped on the chest for the actual assault.

ment, in case the Germans used chemical weapons against them. The issue of clothing had been considerably reduced after the Italian campaign, resulting in the winter equipment, the summer and winter service dresses being returned to the depots.

The equipment issued to the men of the first wave was restricted to what they could carry (see table on page 116). Everything else was packed up in a 'blanket roll' and stored away into unit transport to be delivered with the second wave. For the landing, each man was issued with an extra three pairs of socks. Unnecessary items were shipped back home for safe-keeping.

The Landings Uniform

The equipment worn by some GIs for the amphibious operation is displayed on the model on the left. The man wears an **M1 helmet (1)**, coated with non-reflective paint and adorned with the divisional insignia. The steel shell is worn over a fibre liner, the thin leather chin strap of which is slipped over the front rim. The shell web chin strap has been shortened and is strung over the back of the shell. The chin strap was stitched on hinged metal loops, a stronger arrangement than on the previous welded types. A British Army fine mesh net has been obtained for added camouflage.

The field uniform shown here was introduced at the start of the European conflict. It consists of woollen trousers and shirt plus a field jacket. It is worn under **M-1943 Herringbone twill (HBT) 'fatigues'** **(2 & 3)**, rendered 'protective' by impregnation with an anti-vesicant chemical. This impregnated uniform left unpleasant memories among those who wore it; made clammy, heavy and foul smelling by the chemicals, it also stifled the soldier. Contemporary D-Day documents show that the GIs usually shed the jacket before their trousers. The unlined jacket had six black metal buttons down the front, and two plastic ones were sewn under the turn down collar at the back to secure a gas-proof hood. For increased protection against chemical weapons, a rectangular flap was stitched inside the left side panel of the jacket and secured to the right one by three buttons. The cuffs were gathered by two buttonholes in the bottom hem. The straight trousers had five fly buttons. A triangular, buttoned gas flap was sewn on the inside of the fly. The trousers were secured by the regulation belt. The large cargo pockets on the chest and thighs were characteristic of the HBT Two-piece uniform; they had rectangular buttoned flaps, and were liked for the large quantity of items they could contain. The manufacturer's label was stitched inside. The garments have no other pockets.

The bottom of the legs were tucked into sturdy canvas leggings (**M-1938 for dismounted troops**) **(4)**. Also impregnated with an anti-gas chemical for the invasion, they were secured by a side lacing, eight hooks and eyelets and held down on the shoe by a bottom strap with a brass buckle. Markings were inked inside the shaft. The **'flesh side out' shoes (5)** had seven eyelets; black rubber heels and soles, and a steel shank between the soles to support the arch. The shoes were impregnated with a special anti-gas chemical for the assault. The markings were stamped inside the shoe.

The Combat Uniform

Introduced shortly before the outbreak of war, and practically unchanged until 1945, the regulation field uniform (*overleaf*) was worn under the gas-proofed HBT Two-piece suit. It was also worn by itself on D-Day, the wool shirt and trousers being impregnated. Photographic evidence proves this was the uniform of most first wave assault troops

111

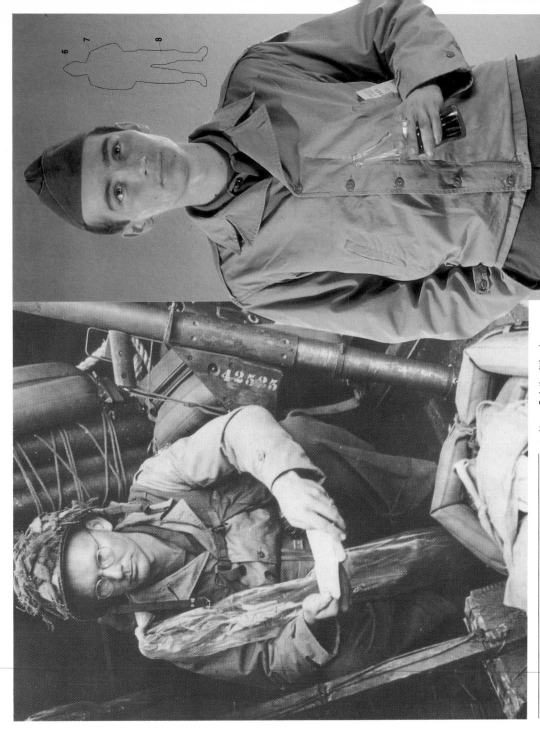

The GI of D-DAY

on D–Day. The protective HBT uniform most mostly issued to non-assault troops.

The **Garrison cap (6)** was issued to all servicemen in 1939. Not included in the invasion kit, the cap was worn by many GIs as, apart from the helmet liner, no comfort headgear was provided. The piping was light blue for the infantry.

The **Field jacket (7)** was evolved from research initiated in 1935 when a replacement for the fourpocket woollen tunic as a combat uniform was needed. Derived from a civilian windbreaker, it could be easily mass-produced. The jacket was tested until 1940 and was standardised in 1941. It was officially known to the Quartermaster Corps as a 'field jacket'. Made of windproof, water repellent cotton poplin, the jacket was fully lined with brown flannel. The front zipper was covered by a flap securing with five plastic buttons. A sixth button kept the lapel in place to close the garment up to the neck. When turned up, the collar was secured by a buttoned tab. The shoulder tabs and fastening straps on the cuffs and hips were also secured with buttons. Loose fitting, the jacket had two back comfort pleats and two slanted inside front pockets. The manufacturer's label was stitched inside one of the pockets.

The **Olive Drab trousers (8)** were derived from the breeches which they replaced in 1933. Cut in wool serge cloth, they were issued to most branches of the Army in 1938 and meant to be worn with leggings for field dress. The fly has five plastic buttons. The trousers had two side and two back poc-

Above: Quietly sitting in a landing craft, this infantryman belongs to the assault troops of D-day. He is clad in the regulation combat uniform, although his trouser legs are worn outside the gaiters, thus negating their protective effect in case of gas attack. Issued to first wave troops as a replacement for the haversack, the assault jacket with its numerous pockets is noteworthy. The equipment piled around the man is representative of the paraphernalia required for amphibious assault: Bangalore torpedoes, lifebelts for added buoyancy of important equipment, demolition and pole charges and an M-1 rocket launcher.

Right: A few days before 'Overlord', Private Lawrence was pictured as he left the PX. Entertainment was scarce in the barracks where the GIs were confined before being shipped to the southern England departure bases. This private's field uniform was worn in action on the beachhead, the woollen clothing being impregnated against vesicatory gases. Introduced shortly before the war, this uniform was criticised by soldiers who felt that the jacket was too warm in summer and did not protect against the cold in winter. Besides, the jacket was prone to soiling, and its pockets were not deep enough. These serious drawbacks notwithstanding, the jacket remained on regular issue until 1945 due to the difficulties of supplying the new green cotton M-1943 Field uniform.

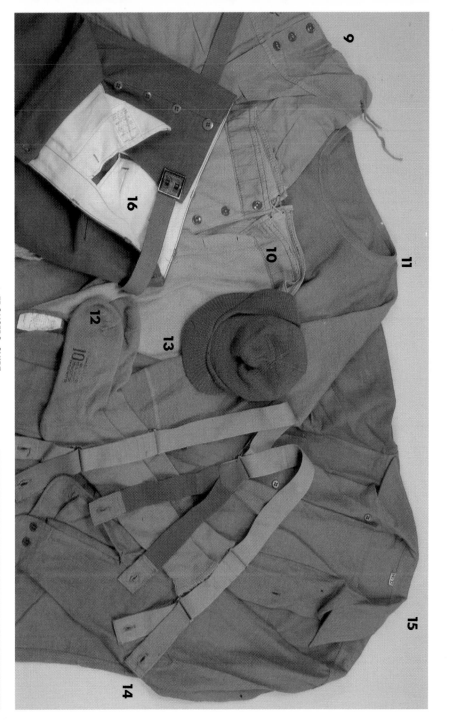

kets. A small fob pocket was provided on the right front. The pockets were cut in white cotton cloth. The trousers issued for the invasion were called 'special' to indicate that they had an anti-gas fly flap.

The **Olive drab shirt** (*bottom right*) was made of brown flannel wool. Introduced in 1934, it superseded the previous pullover-type model, and by 1941, had a 'convertible' collar which could be worn unbuttoned or with a tie. The front had seven buttons, and two patched pockets with straight edged flaps. The shirt was modified when a whole range of gas-proof clothing was introduced in 1943: the cuffs received an additional tightening button and sleeve gussets; a buttoned chest gas flap and two buttons behind the collar to secure the protective wool hood. The unit insignia was sewn on top of the left sleeve in compliance with orders issued by the unit commander.

Underwear

A wide variety of underwear (*see photo above*) was issued by the Quartermaster. Worn in layers so as to provide maximum warmth through insulation, issue underwear (underpants and cotton undershirt) was distributed along with long johns and long-sleeved wool/cotton knitwear. Varying amounts of wool and cotton made up the texture of the fabric which was available in two colours: green and white.

Tightened at the hips by laces, the **short underpants (9)** were made of cotton poplin. The fly had three plastic or mother-of-pearl buttons. The **long johns (10)** were adjusted at the back with a lace and eyelet arrangement.

The **long sleeved undershirt (11)** was very like an ordinary civilian model with a wide opening for the head. The **socks (12)** were made of wool and cotton, and were impregnated with anti-gas chemical for the actual assault.

The **M-1941 wool knit cap (13)** was often worn under the helmet, but was not actually part of the assault troops' uniform.

► TROUSERS, SHIRT AND UNDERWEAR
9. 'Drawers, cotton, shorts'.
10. 'Drawers, wool'.
11. 'Undershirt, wool'.
12. 'Socks, wool, light'.
13. 'Cap, wool, knit, M-1941'. The size is indicated on the label sewn inside the crown. The side flap could be lowered over the ears and nape for warmth.
14. 'Suspenders, trousers' made of cotton and elasticated material, worn with some patterns of wool trousers, not shown here.
15. 'Shirt, flannel, od, coat style, special' with inner gas flap on the chest, sleeve gussets, and two buttons behind the collar to secure the wool protective hood.
16. Trousers, wool serge, od, light shade, special'. The triangular anti-gas flap and the pocket label are noteworthy. The blackened brass open face belt buckle is an early type.

▼ *Right.*
Details of the shirt and wool trousers. The collar is undone, showing the chest gas flap. The pockets and their flaps are typical. The fob gusset at the front appeared on almost all American regulation trousers.

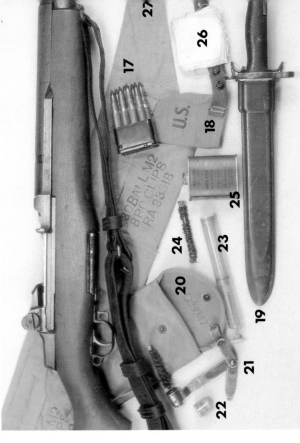

Toiletries

To keep the GIs well groomed, Uncle Sam lavishly provided them with a wide range of toiletries *(below)*. GIs could also buy from the Post Exchange their favourite brands of soap, toothpaste etc. The **toiletry bag (28)** was often provided by the Red Cross. The **shaving cream (29)** was used along with the razor (stamped 'US Army property') and the haemostatic stick. The **toothbrush (30)** is carried in a plastic container besides which a tooth powder can is displayed. Below, a **talcum powder box (31)**, general use soap besides a black plastic soap box and a comb. A nail file, a canvas wash basin and two towels ('Towel Bath' at left and 'Towel, huck', at right) complete the toiletry set.

The GI of D-DAY

Armament

The 30.06 semi-automatic Garand M-1 rifle *(above)* was introduced in 1936. Fed by eight-round *en bloc* clips **(17)**, the weapon was appreciated by its users in spite of its complex maintenance. More than four million Garands were produced during the war by Springfield Armory and Winchester. The weapon is shown with some of its accessories: the **canvas muzzle cover (18)** with pressure stud for securing around the barrel. The **M-1 bayonet (19)** with parkerised blade is carried in a plastic scabbard and hooked to the belt. The cleaning kit is subdivided into two sets carried in the rifle butt and in an oilcloth bag. The kit comprises a **take-down tool (21)**, a **tin of special grease** to lubricate moveable parts **(22)** and a **plastic oiler (23)** which contains the **pull-through (24)**. Cleaning the breech was done with **cotton squares (26)** dipped into the **cleaning fluid (25)**. The cleaning fluid bottle could be carried in one of the cartridge belt pouches. The **bandoleer (27)** has 'Boyt 1942' stamped on its strap.

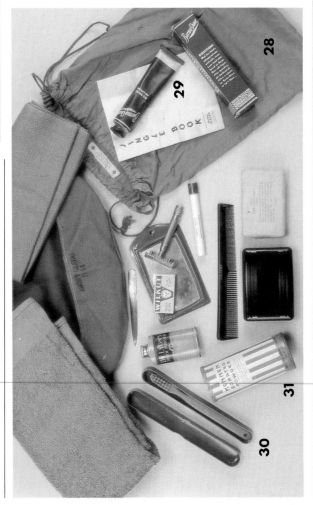

Typical GI paraphernalia displayed on a map showing the operational sector of the 29th ID in June and July 1944:
32. Camera.
33. Money belt.
34. English-French conversation manual.
35. Writing pad, deck of cards and Army driver's licence.
36. Shoe dubbin.
37. Pictures of girlfriends, London tube tickets.
38. Field Manual FM 21-100, The 'Soldier's handbook'.
39. Armed Services Edition paperback, from a non-profit series for servicemen posted overseas.
40. Sewing kit.
41. Watch and religious book.
42. Writing pad and ID tags.
43. Soldier's diary.
44. Tobacco pouch, pipe and tobacco pipe, lighter fuel, issue cigarettes and matches.

Individual Equipment

All individual equipment was arranged around the **M-1923 cartridge belt (45)** which had 10 pressure studded pockets containing one Garand ammo clip each. The belt had two rows of eyelets running along its length; the top one to attach the haversack straps, and the bottom one for the hooks securing the equipment. The **M-1928 haversack (46)** had a back pocket for the mess tin. One the pack's closure straps holds the entrenching tool's handle. Too short to be properly secured to the side of the haversack, the **M-1 bayonet (47)** was often hooked to the cartridge belt. The M-1910 canteen and cup are carried in an **M-1910 canvas cover (48)** lined with wool scraps. A small metal box containing the first aid packet is carried in the **M-1924 pouch (49)**. The set is completed by **M-1938 wirecutters (50)** in their carrier.

Displayed on the blanket *(right)* are a shelter half with its guy line, wooden pins and folding pole kit. The rubberised raincoat has five buttons down the front. One of several models on regular issue, it has pockets, an anti-gas flap, a vent in the back and three ventilation eyelets under the armpits. The Navy M-1926 rubber life belt can be blown up by mouth or more quickly inflated by the two CO_2 gas

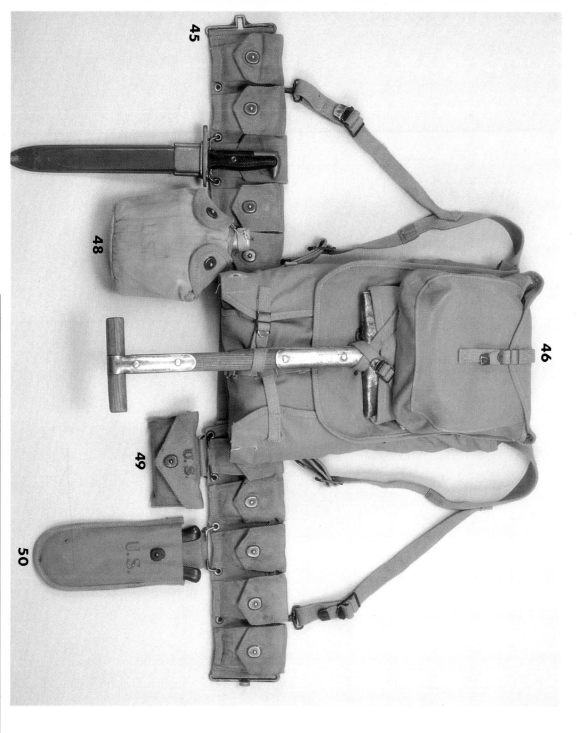

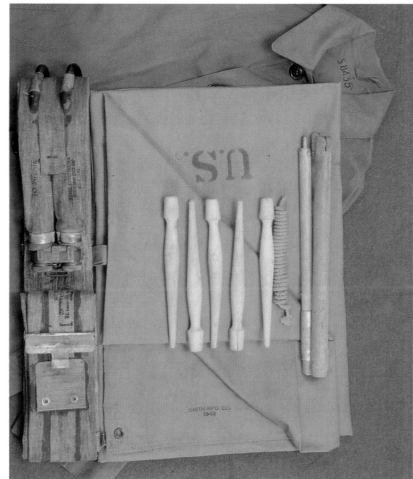

EQUIPMENT ISSUED TO ASSAULT TROOPS FOR OPERATION 'NEPTUNE' (D-DAY TO D-DAY + 44) (1)

● **Items Carried by the Soldier**

- one web belt.
- woollen long johns.
- one pair of impregnated gloves.
- two handkerchiefs.
- one steel helmet.
- one woollen anti-gas protective hood.
- one field jacket.
- one pair of impregnated leggings.
- one impregnated wool shirt.
- one pair of service shoes.
- one pair of impregnated socks.
- one pair of impregnated wool trousers.
- one woollen undershirt.

● **Items Carried in Unit Transport**

- two blankets.
- one pair of short underpants.
- two handkerchiefs.
- one HBT jacket.
- tent pins.
- one pair of service shoes.
- two pairs of woollen socks.
- one shelter half and folding pole.
- one towel.
- one pair of HBT trousers.
- one cotton undershirt

● **Equipment Carried by the Soldier**

- one cartridge belt.
- one canteen.
- one cup.
- one haversack.
- one first aid packet pouch.
- two ID tags.

● **Haversack Contents**

- one meat can.
- one bottle of Halazone water-purifying pills.
- two handkerchiefs.
- four heat tablets.
- one tin of louse powder.
- one raincoat.
- three pairs of light woollen socks.
- one pair of impregnated socks.
- one spoon.
- toiletries.
- one 'Towel, huck'.

(1) 'Neptune' was the codename of the amphibious phase of 'Overlord'. The assault troops included the infantry divisions and the attached armoured, tank destroyer, reconnaissance and field artillery units.

116

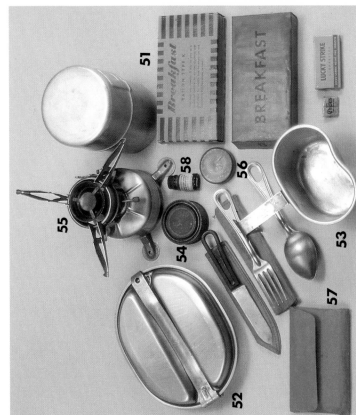

Rations

After being delivered ashore, the troops would be cut off from their back up units and so had to carry enough rations to see them through one day of combat. Designed for such conditions, **K-Rations (51)** were widely distributed to the men. The K-Ration consisted of three meals (breakfast, supper and dinner), each in its own cardboard box. Containing the two packages making up one meal, each box had a distinctive colour and inner waxed wrapping. The breakfast ration contained biscuits, tinned meat, fruit jelly, chewing gum, instant coffee, lumps of sugar and four cigarettes. The meals could be eaten hot or cold, but there is little doubt that warming them up in the **stainless steel 'meat can' (52)** would make them more palatable. Hot water could also be used to make a well-earned brew in the issue **cup (53)**. To cater for his needs, every man was issued with heating tablets or a **wood alcohol can (54)** which he used unless he had managed to secure a **gasoline stove (55)** (shown here is the lighter M-1942 with its aluminium container). **Halazone water purifying tablets (58)** and **candles (56)** were also issued for cooking and lighting, along with **toilet paper (57)** in a waterproof wrapper. The M-1926 cutlery set was carried in the haversack meat can pouch (only by follow-up troops after D-day. Assault troops only kept the spoon). The fork and knife were protected in a leather sheath so as to reduce the wear on the haversack pouch.

bottles fitted at the end of each flange. Inflating by mouth is achieved through two tubes fitted with one-way valves.

The GI of D-DAY

Left: Medical Equipment
59. M-1924 pouch for Carlisle Model First aid packet. The pouch also holds Sulfadiazine (early antibiotics) tablets.
60. Field dressing in waxed cardboard box, usually carried by medics.
61. Carlisle model First aid packet in tin container.
62. Sulfamide powder dispenser (in the tin).
63. Field dressing (held in tin).
64. Louse powder box.
65. Foot powder bag.

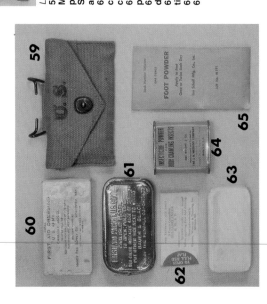

Anti-gas Equipment

Fearing that the Germans might use poison or tear gas against the assault troops, the Americans issued their men with gas detector armbands (brassards). The wearer was immediately alerted to the presence of vesicant gases when the **armband (66)** changed colour. Protection against tear gas which affects the mucous membranes of the lungs and nose was provided by the gas mask. Before the amphibious operation, the Chemical Warfare Service (responsible for poison gas production and protection) evolved the **M5 gas mask (67)** which was lighter than the regular issue M4. The M5 was carried in an **M7 black rubber bag (68)**. The canister (fitting on the cheek) is protected from the water by a rubber seal. The glasses were cleaned with a special **anti-dim cloth (69)** carried in its tube. To ward off the threat of vesicatory gases, the GIs' uniforms were impregnated with chemicals and worn as precaution during the landing. The boots were also coated with protective 'Impregnate Shoe **(70)** before boarding the ships. If exposed to a gas attack, each man had to don his cellophane anti-gas cape, **'Cover, protective, individual'**, his **'Hood, protective, wool' (71 & 72)** and his **'Eye-shields', M1' (73)**. Blisters resulting from exposure to chemicals had to be treated with **'Ointment, protective, M4'** *(bottom left)* applied with the cotton wool wad supplied with the ointment. Most of these items were carried in the gas mask bag.

The author wishes to thank T. Bernard, J. Gawne, J-Y. Nasse, C. Deschodt, P. Besnard as well as the 'Optas' and 'Le Poilu' Militaria shops in Paris for their assistance. For further reading: 'American assault troops in Normandy', by Jon Gawne, in Militaria n° 5 (June 1994 issue).

Right: 6 June 1944: late in the afternoon. *'Marsch, Marsch!'* HJ Division's armour rolls westward. SS-Untersharführer Kretzschmar stands in the turret of a PzKpfw IV Ausf H of the tank regiment's 5th company. On his left is SS-Sturmmann Gaude, the gun loader, and on his right, SS-Sturmmann Schweinfest, the gun layer. The man at the front is SS-Sturmmann Stefan, the radio operator. When the picture was taken, Jabos were on the prowl forcing the vehicles to keep 100m apart so as to reduce vulnerability from air attacks. (ECPA)

Below:
Fritz Witt, pictured at the time he held the rank of SS-Obersturmbannführer. Aged only 35, Witt was commanding one of Nazi Germany's finest divisions. He led the cream of German youth to combat before dying a soldier's death in Normandy.

THE 'HITLERJUGEND' DIVISION IN NORMANDY

A portfolio compiled by
Christophe Deschodt, Jean de Lagarde
and Eric Lefèvre

ACKNOWLEDGEMENTS

The authors and editorial staff wish to thank Monsieur Legrand who kindly put his property and superbly restored vehicles at the disposal of Militaria magazine during outdoor picture sessions. Militaria also expresses its gratitude to the numerous collectors who kindly helped with the project - particularly Dr. J.F. Borsarello and Rémi Theys.

This portfolio is meant to be a pictorial record and, as such, is part of a series devoted to World War 2 fighting forces, the first part of which focused on American paratroopers in Normandy

120

THE 'HITLERJUGEND' DIVISION IN NORMANDY

The original idea of creating a large Waffen-SS unit with Hitlerjugend (Hitler Youth) volunteers rests with NSDAP Reichsjugendführer Artur Axmann and SS-Gruppenführer Gottlob Berger, head of SS-Hauptamt, the body tasked with recruiting personnel for the Waffen-SS.

The two men met in Berlin on 16 February 1943, and decided that youths born in the first half of 1926 - who were therefore aged between 16 1/2 and 17 - were eligible for service with the unit.

In 1939, it was compulsory for all young Germans aged between 10 and 18 to join the NSDAP youth movement [1] even though its activities had become increasingly military-minded. By the end of the thirties, subjects such as shooting, topography and driving were taught. Hitler ordered that camps (*Wehrertüchtigungslager or WEL*) be created so that Hitler Youth members aged 16 1/2 could receive pre-military training from Heer (Army) or Waffen-SS personnel. Already by 1943, many HJ teenagers were serving as auxiliaries with Flak units.

The decision of turning boys into soldiers matched the 'total war' concept which was then being fostered in embattled Germany. Around that time, the German High Command was toying with the idea of incorporating youths into the Heer's active services until the army lost precedence to the Waffen-SS which, for a number of years, had welcomed HJ volunteers into its ranks.

Left: March 1944, on the Beverlo training ground in Flanders during the first exercise involving the various units of the division. OB-West C-in-C Generalfeldmarschall Gerd von Rundstedt attended the manoeuvre. The marshall is seen saluting SS-Obersturmführer Schrott commanding 7.SS-Pz.Gren.-Regt.25 (on the right with outstretched arm), while a platoon leader transferred from the Wehrmacht gives the military salute. (H.P. Taylor).

1 The Nazi Youth Movement included the general HJ for boys aged from 14 to 18; the Deutsches Jungvolk for boys aged from 10 to 14; the Bund Deutscher Mädel in der HJ (Federation of Young German Girls) for girls aged 14 years up; and the Jungmädelbund for girls under 14. Specialised tuition in driving, signals, gliding and sea navigation was provided by four major sub-groups: Motor-HJ, Nachrichten-HJ, Flieger-HJ and Marine-HJ. In addition, the HJ contributed to the war effort, especially in the civil defence field.

With or Without Parental Agreement

Although the youths were under age, they did not need their parents' approval before enlisting. A recruiting schedule and a training programme were soon established. Initially, only volunteers complying with strict physical requirements were retained. Minimum height for infantry was set at 1.70m, and great emphasis placed on ideological motivation. The first batch of 30,000 volunteers promised by Axman was to spend six weeks in a WEL under Waffen-SS leadership before devoting four weeks to the RAD (Reichsarbeitsdienst) compulsory labour service. A four-month military period spent in a Waffen-SS unit would turn the recruits into fully fledged soldiers.

Axman urged local authorities to hasten the recruiting procedures as his proposal had met with approval at the highest level - the Führer Adolf Hitler was enthusiastic about the project. Reichsführer SS Himmler, Axman and Berger intended to turn the new force into an elite unit of the same standard as the famed LSSAH Division (SS Panzer-Division 'Leibstandarte Adolf Hitler').

The project was shrouded in such secrecy that when the recruiting campaign was initiated, absolutely no details about the purpose or shape of the future force were given. This stemmed from Doctor Goebbels' fear that the Allies might regard this measure as a last-ditch attempt to make up for the disaster the Germans had suffered at Stalingrad.

Recruiting, however, proved harder than expected: many parents objected to their sons enlisting and did

The 'Hitlerjugend' Division

their best to dissuade them from joining. In addition, many recruits were not tall enough or fell short of fitness requirements. This soon led to a rumour that boys were being dragooned into service. In May 1943, the first 8,000 volunteers were directed to WELs for an amended shorter training period (four weeks instead of six) and exempted from the compulsory labour stint.

The Spirit and Leadership of the Leibstandarte

The division was officially raised on 1 June 1943 in compliance with an order issued by SS-Führungshauptamt (Waffen-SS High Command) dated 24 June. The new unit was a motorised infantry division (Panzergrenadier-Division) and quite naturally named 'Hitlerjugend'.

Most of the divisional officer corps was made up of reserve officers. Numbering some 400, these officers were HJ leaders who had been detached from the Luftwaffe, the Heer and the Waffen-SS. Infantry and artillery commissions at battalion, company or battery level, were allocated to experienced LSSAH officers. The Division's C-in-C, 35-year-old Oberführer Fritz Witt, also came from the Leibstandarte. Other old hands made up the framework of the new division, and imparted their fighting spirit and particular ethos to the recruits. In addition, a further 120 LSSAH officers arrived in June, followed later by several hundred NCOs. In some instances, whole companies, tank crews, gunners, recce or medical personnel were drafted into the division from

Left: Another shot taken on 6 June 1944: a light SdKfz 10/4 tractor towing a 20mm Flak AA gun rumbles through the main street of Saint-Pierre-sur-Dives. This vehicle might have been on strength with either SS-Pz.Regt-26 or with the air defence platoon detailed to HQ protection. (ECPA)

RELIVING HISTORY THROUGH RE-ENACTMENT

It is hard to believe that the hands of time haven't turned back. More than four decades later, the colours suddenly burst into life again. Bags crammed with original WW2 uniforms and equipment, the Militaria Magazine team has come to Normandy. Foliage from trees that stood there during the battle itself was used to cover the vehicles so superbly restored by Monsieur Legrand. If the walls and tiles could talk, they would say: *'Yes: that's quite the way things were!'*

Our time machine stopped at a more precise date - 11 June 1944. On that day, the 'Hitlerjugend' Panzerdivision was relieved after having lived through over a month of desperate fighting. Its rest was cut short when, on 18 June the British launched Operation 'Goodwood', an offensive of unprecedented might. The division's tactical groups left their rest areas before proceeding towards the front line where their comrades of the battered 21st Panzerdivision anxiously waited for relief.

The stage was now set and the big show could start.
Action!

this unit was ferried to Flanders and took up quarters at Hasselt).

— A rocket launcher battalion (Werferabteilung) created at Sterzing (southern Tyrol) then transferred to Belgium in winter before moving on to Enghien (France).

— An assault-gun battalion (Panzer-Sturmgeschützabteilung) later converted into a anti-tank battalion after being issued with self propelled anti-tank guns.

In spite of the recruiting difficulties, some 12,472 men had been mustered by the end of September. Officers, however, were still scant and numbered only 183. The division always suffered from a shortage of officers even though a further 50 were commissioned from the Heer into HJ (mostly engineer officers and heavy weapon specialists).

High on Spirit But Low on Fuel!

In its early days, the division was critically short of materiel and heavy weapons as typified by the tank regiment which only had three tanks on 1 October, and 10 on 1 November (of this number, four were PzKpfw IVs and two were obsolescent PzKpfw IIIs purloined from the Alkett plant in Berlin). There were practically no trucks, no armoured cars, no half tracks and no motorbikes. In December 1943, Italian-made lorries and light trucks trickled in along with the first armoured cars of the recce battalions. The Italian vehicles, how-ever, tended to be inferior to German designs and were anything but reliable. The quantity of fuel and ammunition allocated for exercises was also poor and unsufficient.

HJ command soon had another problem to solve: turning thousands of often physically and mentally immature youths into soldiers. This was a daunting task despite the young men's enthusiasm for weapons and military equipment which far exceeded that of their elders. Later, weekly rations were increased and, in spite of

Above:
A wartime picture taken at Bueil, a small village in the Eure department, where some 'Hitlerjugend Division' units were quartered before the Allies landed in Normandy. Now belonging to SS-Pz.Gren.-Regt.26, the three young men hail from the 'Leibstandarte' as their cuff bands indicate. The variety of uniforms is noteworthy as it includes camouflage material of Italian origin, field grey and 1944 Pattern camouflage uniforms. Of the three young men shown here, two never returned to Germany: only SS-Sturmmann Günther Quiel (right) survived the horror of the Normandy Campaign.

Right:
Waffen-SS soldiers in the same attitudes, uniforms, and vehicles as in 1944. The half-track shown here is a medium Schützenpanzerwagen (SdKfz 250, early type built until October 1943). The half-track can accommodate six men: half a rifle section plus the driver. Armoured recce units used to be at the spearhead even though - as in the photograph - they were sometimes bolstered by panzergrenadiers. On the left stands the machine-gun N°2 carrying belted ammunition in a box (300 rounds). The gunner sits on the bonnet cradling his MG. 42. The infantryman on the right holds a Tellermine 'Pilz' (mushroom) anti-tank mine supplied by engineers to cover the unit during withdrawal.

The 'Hitlerjugend' Division

the LSSAH. In July, eligibility for serving with the division was extended to youths born in the second half of 1926. These newcomers were also exempted from compulsory labour while, 'for practical reasons', pre-military training was no longer provided in WELs but in divisional quarters.

In July and August 1943, some 10,000 volunteers gathered on the Beverlo training ground in occupied Flanders, some 72km south-west of Antwerp, where the division was being raised.

The organisation and training of the division's sub-units lasted until early 1944 in the following Flanders garrisons:

— Beverlo: on 20 July 1943, creation of two motorised infantry regiments (one was deployed as soon as ready on the Mariater Heide training ground, about 15km north east of Antwerp).

— Mol and surroundings (near Beverlo): an artillery regiment raised on 5 September.

— Turnhout (48km north-east of Antwerp): a recce battalion raised on 4 September, a medical battalion raised on 5 September and a signals battalion.

— Herentals (on the Albert canal): an engineer battalion.

— Geel and surroundings (50km east of Antwerp): a motorised supply battalion and support battalion created on 20 July.

The Panzergrenadiers' training and replacement battalion (SS-Pz. Gren.-A.u.E. Btl. 12) was barracked at Arnhem in the Netherlands.

The 'HJ' Becomes a Panzerdivision

The 'Hitlerjugend' became a full-sized armoured division in compliance with Hitler's directive of 21 October 1943 which specified that all divisions answering to I and II Panzerkorps were to be raised to armoured division status. Ten days later, following an order from SS-FHA, the unit became officially known as 12th SS-Panzerdivision 'Hitlerjugend', and was organised and staffed like 1943-type regular army Panzerdivision [2].

Additional units were then raised and consolidated within the division:

— A maintenance group (specialising in armoured vehicles) raised on 1 November and quartered at Turnhout.

— A command protection company raised on the same day in the same garrison.

— A tank regiment, created on 3 November on the Mailly-le-Camp training ground in France (in January,

2. HJ was not patterned like standard 1944 Panzerdivisions.

Right:
Late July or early August. Heavily covered in foliage, men and machine blend in with the Normandy landscape. The typical silhouette of a medium Schützenpanzerwagen SdKfz 251 can be distinguished under the foliage from which protrudes a gun barrel. This weapon, a French built 25mm AA machine-gun, is known to have occasionally replaced the heavy anti-tank rifles (s.Pz.B.41) fitted to vehicles of 1. Pz.-Komp. of SS-Pz.-Pionier-Batl.12. (Picture: ECPA).

125

Right: The routes have now been carefully plotted. Orders are transmitted by radio to HJ units. Ciphers were often used and the frequencies changed to confuse enemy radio monitoring stations. The officer is using a portable Tornister-Funkgerät d2 set installed in the Schwimmwagen. It is late July and the sun is hot: the men wear no shirts under their tunics.

wartime restrictions, HJ recruits had a richer diet than labourers doing heavy work. Most of the junior officers were under 25 who, given the nature of their responsibilities, often acted as substitutes for mobilised or dead fathers. Relationships with the youths were informal: in all their dealings with their men, officers tended to behave like big brothers or mature comrades. This particular spirit was well illustrated in the way misdemeanours were punished. The teenagers were still children and so training was not confined to quarters but often took place out in the open with more emphasis being placed on sport than drill.

Three men were responsible for the successful way the division was raised: SS-Oberführer Witt, SS-Standartenführer Kurt Meyer - the legendary 'Panzermeyer' - commanding SS-Pz. Gren.-Rgt. 25; and SS-Obersturmbannführer Wünsche, the commanding officer of SS-Pz.Rgt.12. These officers were living examples to the young recruits who regarded their valour and dash as a source of inspiration.

By 1943, the initial training phase of the first intake was over. Exercises could be conducted at combat group, section and platoon level. In early 1944, most of the heavy equipment had been delivered: 100mm and 150mm howitzers, 75mm anti-tank guns, MG-42 machine-guns, German-built trucks, motorcycles and even Schützenpanzer half-tracks. In February, the tank regiment fielded 97 PzKpfw IVs - but only had eight Panthers, then the best medium tank in the German inventory.

April 1944:
The Division Is Ready

The first combined exercise involving tank battalions and panzergrenadiers took place in March on the Beverlo training ground. The event was attended by Generalfeldmarschall Gerd von Rundstedt, Commander-in-Chief or OB West (Oberbefehlshaber-West - supreme commander, Western Command).

In April, I SS-Panzerkorps command considered that the HJ Division was *einsatzbereit* (combat ready), even though most of its shortcomings had yet to be overcome, particularly its allotment of motor vehicles. On 1 March, the establishment of HJ stood at 16,139 men, of whom only 430 were officers. Patiently honed

Below: 6 June 1944: a fateful day which will be etched for ever in the minds of those who lived through it. A 'Wespe' (wasp) 100mm self-propelled howitzer on regular issue to 1st and 2nd batteries of SS-Pz.-Artillerie-Regt.12 rumbles westward after crossing the village of Saint-Pierre-sur-Dives. The crew's packs are secured to the gun's armour. In keeping with regulations, these 'armoured gunners' have been issued with standard uniforms (overalls were on exclusive issue to the crews of specific vehicles). The HJ formation sign is visible on the right hand side of the glacis.

The 'Hitlerjugend' Division

over nine months of training, the division was transferred to Normandy to await future deployments. In the first fortnight of April 1944, 90 trains ferried the Hitlerjugend Division to its new quarters. The unit was scattered over a wide zone overlapping five French departments: Eure, Calvados, Orne, Eure-et-Loir and the former Seine-et-Oise. HJ was deployed as follows:

— HQ at the Château du Rousset-d'Acon.
— SS-Pz.Rgt.12: around Elbeuf, le Neubourg and Louviers (for rapid deployment on both banks of the Seine).
— SS-Pz.Gren.-Rgt.25: around Bernay, Orbec, Vimoutiers and Sées (for rapid intervention in the Caen-Falaise sector).
— SS-Pz.Gren.-Rgt.26: around Houdan.
— SS-Pz.Aufkl.-Abt.12: around Rugles.
— SS-Pz.Art.-Rgt.12: around Damville.
— SS-Werfer-Abt.12: around Mantes-la-Jolie, then on to Dreux and Nonencourt.
— SS-Pz.Jäger-Abt.12: around Nogent-le-Roi.
— SS-Flak-Abt.12: around Dreux, then around Louviers in May.
— SS-Pz.Pi.Btal.12: around Pacy-sur-Eure and Autheuil (to be on hand to carry out engineer work for the Seine crossing).
— SS-Pz.-Nachr.-Abt.12 at Verneuil-sur-Avre and Brézolles.

Along with another three large armoured units quartered in the West, HJ was integrated with OKW's (Oberkommando der Wehrmacht or Wehrmacht's High

SS-Pz.-Div.-Nachschubtr. 12, Wirtschafts-Btl.12, SS-Pz.Inst.-12, SS-San.-Abt.12: around Mortagne in the Orne department.

Left:
The SS-Unterscharführer has replaced his cloth 'Schiffchen' (sidecap) with a camouflage field cap for better protection from the sun. The peak effectively shields his eyes as he carefully plots the route and records the co-ordinates of hamlets on the map. He then turns around to ensure that the message has been transmitted and its receipt acknowledged. This 'Leibstandarte' veteran has been credited with the destruction of an enemy tank, as indicated by the insignia on his right upper sleeve. Quite exceptionally for an NCO, he has also been awarded the German Cross in Gold and wears the embroidered version of this medal on the right chest pocket of his tunic.

Command) tactical reserves on 29 April.

The tempo of training accelerated in April and May. Most exercises took place at night as the general feeling was that action was drawing closer. The teenage soldiers concentrated on camouflage and practised emergency drills - even though fuel was still in short supply. But already, Panzergruppe West had requested from HJ that the access ways to the coast between Caen and the Somme river be reconnoitred.

The 'Baby Division'

The influx of volunteers was such that the division had soon reached its full complement and could afford turning some 2,055 men over to the LSSAH which was then in dire need of manpower. Although not all teething problems had been solved, the division was regarded as fully operational on 1 June 1944, with the exception of two units: the rocket launcher battalion which still hadn't got the tractors it needed to tow its 41 six-barrelled Nebelwerfer, and the anti-tank battalion which only had 10 Jagdpanzer IVs out of the regular complement of 45 (this AFV had been recently introduced). These shortages seriously hampered the training of both units.

As shown in the order of battle (page 157), the HJ Division's equipment cannot be described as outstanding. What made the HJ an exceptional unit was the bravery of the young volunteers which had been honed by prolonged and thorough physical and psychological preparation. Over the airwaves, Allied propagandists often derided what they called the 'Baby Division', some going even as far as suggesting that a feeding bottle be chosen as its insignia. They ignored the fact that the bottle didn't contain milk but nitroglycerine!

The 'Hitlerjugend' Division

Right:
The rifle sections have been delivered near the front line by armoured vehicles. The arrival of advanced elements often indicated that relief was on the way. But where are the friendly units? As often in military operations, uncertainty prevails but this doesn't prevent a young soldier from grinning. After all, these men have been through worse in June, and all the hazards of war are now almost routine.
The soldier in the foreground is issued with the platoon's rifle grenade launcher, which he carries in the leather case slung over his shoulder.

Below:
The same anxious gaze as on the soldier above (left foreground). The bottom photograph was shot on 9 June 1944 at Villeneuve, a small Normandy hamlet between Caen and Bayeux after 1. Komp. of SS-Pz.Gren.-Regt.26 had moved into the village of Rots.

Below right:
Dust coated faces and obscured the camouflage patterns of uniforms. The goggles hanging from the grenadier's neck were on regular issue to motorised infantry units. In blatant disregard for his own safety, the man has slipped a cocked P-38 handgun into his belt. But the enemy is probably closing in...

6 June 1944: 'Codeword: Blücher'

At 3am on 6 June, the first reports of Allied activity reached SS-Brigadeführer Witt who took it upon himself to put the division on full standby. Enthusiastically, the units geared up and were underway under an hour. On orders from OB-West, I Aufkl.Komp. pushed as far as the coast.

Due to procrastination and dithering among the upper echelons, precious time was wasted before the division received the order to assemble before the division reached its assembly area, east of the Orne river, where the Germans expected another landing. Consequently, mustering started at 7am and the order to move was given at 10am.

It was not until 3.05pm that the division was ordered to proceed to another assembly zone but this time south-west of Caen. When the dispatch order was given at 5pm, not all units had reached the area to which they had been directed earlier that day. Travelling over several routes to by pass Caen to the south, the first combat groups reached their departure line at night after losing 83 men to Allied 'Jabo' (Jagdbomber or fighter bomber) attacks.

On 7 June, SS-Pz.Gren.-Rgt.25 carried out a successful - if hastily planned - counter-attack against the spearheads of the Canadian 3rd Infantry Division. In this action, the panzergrenadiers were backed up by PzKpfw IV tanks and 150mm howitzers provided respectively by II.SS-Pz.-Regt.12 and III./SS-Pz.Art.Rgt.-12.

To Die For Caen

Answering to 1 SS-Panzerkorps, the HJ Division was positioned between the 21st Panzer-Division on the right and the Panzer-Lehr Division on the left. Within this deployment stretching over 16km, the young panzergrenadiers launched a few counter-attacks before being involved in defensive fighting of unprecedented ferocity [3]. The teenage soldiers gradually fell back but through their spirited resistance, checked the Anglo-Canadians who did not capture the city of Caen until much later.

When relieved on 11 July, the Division had lost about 1,000 men killed for a grand total of 4,485 casualties. On 14 June the divisional commander, Fritz Witt, was himself killed by a navy shell as he was directing the battle from his command post at the castle of Vernoix. He was replaced by 'Panzermeyer'.

Sent off to the north of Falaise for rest and refit, the division took stock of its equipment and repaired or maintained whatever it had left. It was never restored

Above and below: **Action stations - khaki figures with flat helmets have been spotted. A half-section of rifleman takes up position. The gunner firmly holds the stock of his MG-42 ensuring that it is steady on its bipod. Meanwhile, the loader checks the ammunition belt for a smooth firing feed. The high firing rate of the machine-gun (25-rds/sec) calls for strict fire discipline, acquired through months of training and tested in the field during earlier engagements.**

3. Due to the savage nature of the fighting - matched by the the mettle of the soldiers - both sides committed acts which are condemned by the rules of war. Disregarding their own lives and showing no mercy for their enemy, both the young Germans and the Canadians fought ferociously in a way reminiscent of Far Eastern tradition in which the beaten foe has forfeited any right to consideration.

Far left and left: Then and now or now and then? The infantryman at left wears the 1944 Pattern camouflage uniform with summer equipment. Next, the original photograph of a rifle section leader wearing the same uniform. He is issued with 6x30 binoculars slung high on the chest. It is harvest time as shown by the wheat ears the soldier has slipped through the loops of his helmet cover.

Right
The MG-42 team is still beating up the area as infantrymen explore the buildings. The armament and equipment of the machine-gun team have been recreated with utmost accuracy. The gunner is only armed with a pistol whereas the ammunition carrier at left has a rifle. The latter carries three boxes of belted ammunition and the back 'combat pack'. The two other crewmen have opted for the lightened pack order, as befits men burdened with boxes of ammunition.

The 'Hitlerjugend' Division in Normandy, June 1944

to its former strength [4]. Two combat groups (Kampfgruppen Wünsche and Waldmüller) were created by putting together the units which had retained the highest operational potential.

On 19 July, the division was deployed in the Emiéville-Frénouville sector south-east of Caen when the Allies launched Operation 'Goodwood'. Operating within a deep and skilful defence system, the Germans managed to check the British VIIIth Corps.

Relieved again on 3 and 4 August, the division was deployed as the tactical reserve of I SS-Panzerkorps. It was soon engaged again to the south of Caen where, on 7 August, it delayed the Allies who had launched Operation 'Totalize'. In the 8 and 9 August battles, no fewer than 200 Allied tanks would have been lost in the HJ-held sector alone!

With the exception of support units and elements sent to the rear for refitting, the following forces were at 'Panzermeyer's' disposal on 12 August:

— SS-Pz.Rgt.12: seven Panthers and 17 PzKpfw IVs.
— SS-Pz.Gren.-Rgt.25: two combat companies.
— SS-Pz.Gren.-Rgt.26: four combat companies.
— SS-Pz.Aufkl.Abt.12 (reduced to Wienecke's unit).
— SS-Pz. Art.-Rgt.12: full complement, although II Gruppe had lost two batteries, and I Gruppe was grossly under strength.
— SS-Werfer-Abt.12: three batteries.
— SS-Flak-Abt. 12: one 88 battery; one company of 37 self-propelled guns, and one company of 20 self-propelled guns (14./SS-Pz.Gren.Rgt.26).
— SS-Pz.Jäger-Abt.12: two Jagdpanzer IV companies.
— SS-Pz.-Nachr.-Abt.12 under strength.

This shows that most mechanised infantry regiments had simply melted away. As for the engineer battalion, it had been well and truly annihilated.

On 16 August at Falaise, about 50 'Grenadiere' fought to the last man in the ruins of the girls' high school. From 17 to 19 August, the division's tactical groups carried out a successful delaying action to the south-east of Falaise to keep the Allies from closing the pocket in

Right:
After a leap forward, the group has gathered behind a wall to keep out of sight from the enemy and shelter from direct fire. But fighting in such a tight order as here has its drawbacks: heavier losses would incur should the soldiers come under fire from grenade launchers or mortars. However, the battle-hardened grenadiers will soon deploy to outflank the enemy. The machine-gunner has adopted the firing position used in unexpected combat situations: he has rested the barrel of his weapon on the shoulder of the loader who holds the bipod firmly with both hands. Meanwhile, the man armed with the grenade launcher waits for the order to rush forward with the soldiers kneeling in the foreground. Mismatched uniforms combined with the reshuffle of units in the previous days explains the varied and colourful mixture of the camouflage patterns seen on the men.

4. Of all the German armoured units engaged in Normandy, only 3rd Coy of SS-Pz.Rgt.12 received 17 Panthers at the end of June after losing almost all its tanks in action.

130

the north and trap German forces there. On 20 and 21 August, the same units tried to break through between Trun and Chambois.

By then, the HJ Division had lost some 8,000 men, most of its tanks, self-propelled guns, howitzers and guns. However, the units still numbered about 12,500 men around whom a new division could be raised in a matter of weeks. Irrespective of the Allies' overwhelming might, the young Grenadiers of HJ always held their ground and lost none of their fighting spirit - no mean achievement in view of the odds stacked against them.

□

Kameraden, an die Gewehre!
Denn wo wir auch kommen
Da kennt man uns schon,
Wir Panzergrenadiere
Der H.J. Division.

Take up arms comrades!
For wherever we go,
We are already famous,
We panzergrenadiers of the HJ Division!

Marching song of the HJ Division.

However trite these words may be, they rang awfully true at the end of July 1944. The British and Canadians no longer belittled the 'Baby Division', but had learnt to respect these obdurate soldiers who exacted a heavy price in blood for every inch of ground they yielded. The colours of today's pictures blend with yesteryear's shadows in the mirror of time. The original pictures were taken on 9 June 1944 at Villeneuve, a small hamlet in Normandy.

The 'Hitlerjugend' Division

Left:
An informal shot taken a few seconds before the assault. The advance will be covered by the MG-42 loosing off short bursts at the windows of the buildings behind which the enemy lurks. The section leader waits for the right moment to give the order to attack.

Right:
It's over. The machine-gunner takes a well-earned drink from the water bottle he has unhooked from his breadbag. The SS-Untersharführer looks tense after the engagement: he too had to make use of his MP-40, the weapon on standard issue to platoon leaders.

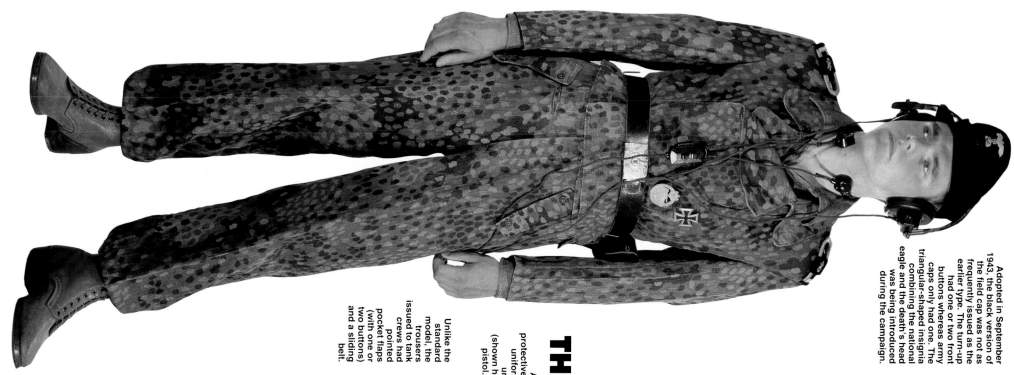

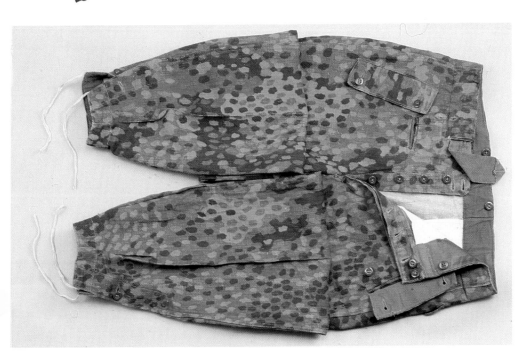

THE CAMOUFLAGE SUIT

An officer of one of the division's tank regiments presents the camouflage protective suit. This uniform was issued to tank crews in 1944. Like the camouflage uniform distributed to other services around that time, it could replace the cloth uniform or be worn over it. In some cases, the standard camouflage pattern (shown here) had no green motif. Like the rest of the crew, the man is armed with a pistol. He wears a B-type headset and a throat microphone of the type issued to tank drivers and loaders, and connected to the tank's intercom.

Adopted in September 1943, the black version of the field cap was not as frequently issued as the earlier type. The turn-up had one or two front buttons whereas army caps only had one. The triangular-shaped insignia combining the national eagle and the death's head was being introduced during the campaign.

Unlike the standard model, the trousers issued to tank crews had pointed pocket flaps (with one or two buttons) and a sliding belt.

of a double-breasted tunic with matching trousers, the uniform was made of 'Schilfgrün' material. Cut and make-up were identical to those of the black field uniform.

(2) Camouflage Overall for Tank Crews *(Kombination, getarnt, für Panzer).*

Adopted in January 1943 as a substitute for the Schützanzug. Designed for the crews of the same vehicles, the 'Kombination' was cut in the same reversible cloth as used for the manufacture of helmet covers, smocks etc. This overall is missing from the 1943 official set of clothing which, oddly enough, still includes the former Schilfgrün suit. This may have been caused by short supplies or by the users' complaints which eventually led to the overall being dropped all together.

(3) Unofficial Uniforms

Although the clothing of armoured forces personnel seems to have been fairly consistent, two non-regulation items of camouflage clothing were issued in 1944 to the tank crews of HJ, LSSAH and I. SS-Panzerkorps organic tank battalion.

- Italian Camouflage Clothing

Available as overalls [1] or as two-piece uniforms cut like the double-breasted cloth tunic and trousers. Many variants were observed (see feature on Italian camouflage cloth items).

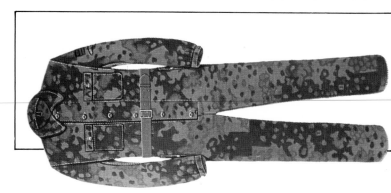

The camouflage overall. Issued in 1943 to the crews of armoured vehicles, shown here with officer rank badges and early army-type belt (Drawing: Eric Lefevre).

- Leather Protective Suit

Made of black leather or ersatz material, this suit consisted of a jacket with matching straight trousers. Initially meant for Kriegsmarine mechanics and stokers serving on board diesel engine-propelled vessels (ships and submarines) [2], this clothing was instead delivered to the Italian Navy. These leather garments were seized in September 1943 by elements the LSSAH Division sent to northern Italy to disarm the Duce's armed forces. According to reports, the requisition was ordered by SS-Ostubaf. Wünsche who would soon take command of HJ's tank regiment.

Original photographs show that the issue of leather clothing was extended to other Waffen-SS armoured formations after being exclusively worn by SS-Panzerkorps' tank crews in summer 1944.

Undeniably awkward in hot weather, leather clothing protected effectively from flash burns. These protective properties had previously been noticed by other armies, particularly the French, who had issued their tank crews with leather coats. SS-Ostubaf. Wünsche probably drew from his own experience when he decided to have the leather uniforms impounded and issued to his crews.

1. The Italian cloth overall was also worn by some panzergrenadiers.
2. The colour of the tank crew uniform was black or dark brown. It is thought to have been intended for mechanics on duty in the engine room. Leather clothing issued to stokehold personnel was grey.

ARMOURED COMBAT DRESS

Left: **When issued to officers, both the field-grey and black double breasted tunics had aluminium braid around the collar. The 'P' gothic ciphers on the shoulder tabs are noteworthy: they were privately purchased from army tailors by Waffen-SS AFV crews who kept on wearing the cipher throughout the war in disregard of official directives.**

Left: The special field grey trousers had the same cut as the black ones.

▼

Right: Two officers in field grey uniforms (purchased from the corps' store and worn with rank badges). In 1944, these uniforms were only issued to the AFV crews of SS-Panzerjäger-Abt. 12, a unit resulting from the transformation of the 1943 assault gun regiment into an AFV unit.

The SS-Ustuf. (left) is seen in the walking-out/service dress. Like the black uniform, the field grey 'Sonderbekleidung' replaces all general issue clothing. This uniform was meant to be worn with a white or light brown poplin shirt, but here again, choice depended on availibility. The man also wears the regulation belt with round buckle as issued to all service branches. The cloth of the trousers has a typical field grey hue, whereas the tunic shows the greyish colour so typical of 1944 Waffen-SS uniforms.

The uniform of the SS-Ostuf (right) is a mixed combination of field grey and Italian cloth as often encountered among personnel on active duty. Issued to all Waffen-SS service branches in 1943, the Feldmütze was only replaced in 1943 (the officers' model had aluminium braiding around the crown).

Transferred from an assault gun unit, the officer has retained the red piping of the artillery to which his service branch answered. Due to a shortage - or selected on account of its sturdiness - the man wears an army officer's belt. His trousers are one of the several types cut in Italian 'tela mimenizatta'.

INSIGNIA AND PERSONAL EFFECTS

A collection of typical HJ documents, headgear and insignia. Regulations stated that when transferred to a unit without emblems, personnel should retain the insignia and badges of their original formation. HJ didn't have its own emblems until autumn 1944 and thus, Leibstandarte shoulder tabs and cuff bands were frequently encountered, as this division had contributed massively to the cadre of HJ division.

1. Pattern 1935 steel helmet, modified in 1942. The 'Sigrune' transfer was dropped in 1943.

2. Officers' peaked cap (non-regulation model derived from the army's 'a/A Feldmütze'.

3. The rare faceveil was strapped around the helmet's shell.

4. 'Panzerkampfabzeichen' combat clasp, shown here in its bronze variant. This badge was awarded to panzergrenadiers and armoured vehicle crews who had fought bravely.

5. ID tag. The tank crew model was secured with a chain - a fireproof material.

6. Ranker's shoulder tab with pink armour/anti-tank piping. The slip-on is adorned with the LAH (Leibstandarte Adolf Hitler) cypher, embroidered in silver grey thread for all service branches. Officers 'mit Portepee' had a gilt cypher and other officers a brass one, pinned in both cases to the shoulder tab.

7. Private's shoulder tab with yellow piping (signals).

8. SS-Uscha. Shoulder tab with scarlet piping as issued to artillery, air defence and rocket launcher units; the grey backing was used only on field uniforms.

9. Rank insignia, worn on garments devoid of shoulder tabs. The printed version shown here is that of an SS-Uscha.

10. SS-Ostuf. shoulder tab with pink piping. Rank pips on officers' shoulder tabs were made of gilt (although December 1939 regulations specified that Waffen-SS rank pips were to be made of bronze, so as to differentiate them from the army's gold ones).

11. SS-Stubaf. shoulder tabs with white piping (panzergrenadier).

12. Variant of death's head insignia. Embroidered in silver thread, it was worn on field headgear by officers and all ranks.

13. SS-Soldbuch (paybook) belonging to a volunteer of SS-Pz.Gren.-Regt.25.

14. Cover of a Soldbuch issued to an HJ Division member in 1943.

15. Early 1936 collar tab variant as issued to officers and other ranks with silver thread embroidered runes.

16. Late variant of collar runes. By 1943, woven runes replaced the embroidered ones.

17. Standard officers' shoulder tabs, with silver thread embroidered 'runes'. The shoulder tab also has aluminium bullion piping. Standard for all uniforms and indicating the rank of SS-Ostuf.

18. Variant of national emblem (Hoheitabzeichen) as issued NCOs and lower ranks. Sewn on the left sleeve, introduced in 1943 and worn along with embroidered insignia.

19. Variant of embroidered national emblem, as issued from 1938 to 1945. Available in several versions. Both types of insignia are embroidered or woven in silver, grey or white thread.

20. Belt buckle issued to NCOs and lower ranks. Made of embossed steel with dull painted finish.

21. 2nd Class Iron Cross award certificate. Awarded to an engineer and signed by the division commander, SS-Staf. Kurt Meyer.

22. Officers' 'Adolf Hitler' cuff band. Early type with silver thread embroidering. The model issued to NCOs and lower ranks was embroidered in grey thread.

23. The Hitler Youth valour award (Leistungsabzeichen der HJ), introduced in 1943, shown here in its bronze version. Awarded to 16-year old boys, early 1943 regulations stipulated that its award gave priority entry to the HJ.

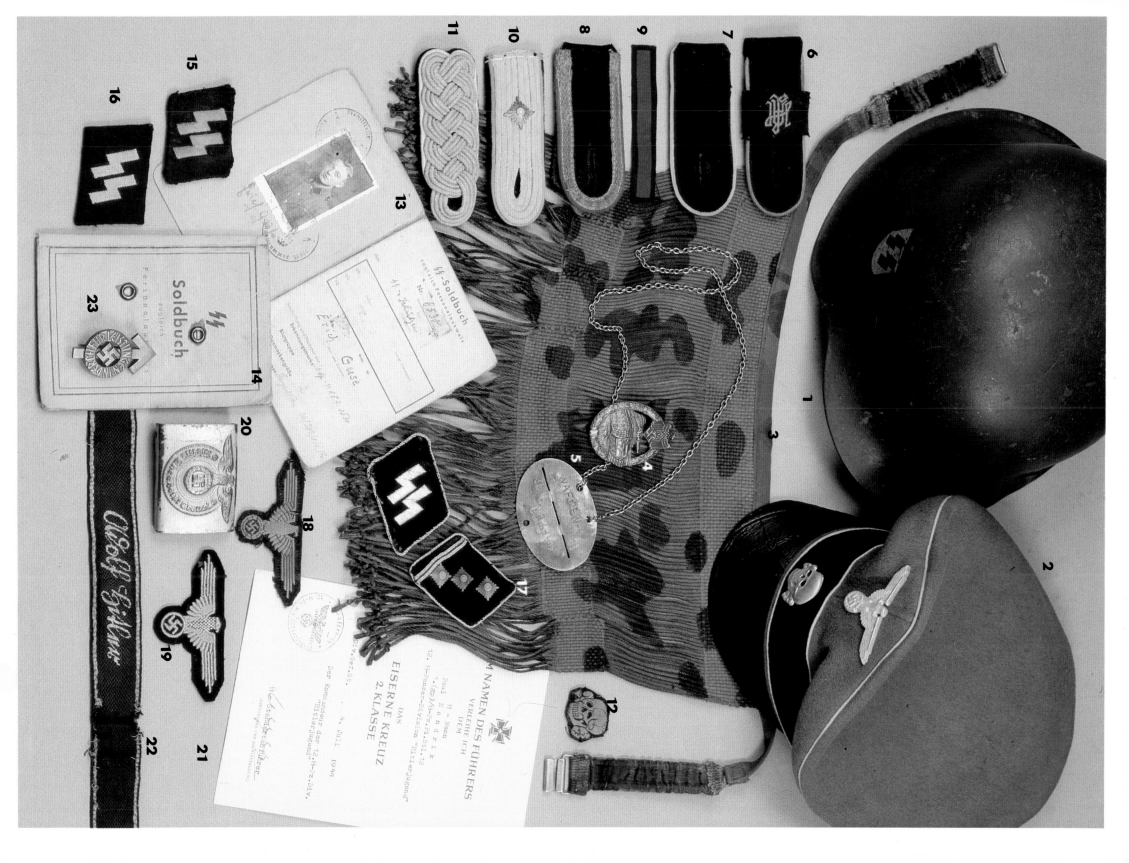

HJ DIVISIONAL INSIGNIA

The divisional insignia was officially carried by all vehicles of the HJ Division. It was selected from among projects submitted by the division staff during a contest run in November 1943. Rules specified that entries would not be accepted after 15 December 1943. The winner was Franz Lang, a staff officer. The notched sinister chief indicates that the unit is an armoured division while the oak leaves under the centre base signify that its commander has been awarded the Knight's Cross 'mit Eichenlaub'.

The charges have the following meanings:

– the 'Sigrune' (a single Gothic letter 'S'): the emblem of the 'Deutsches Jungvolk', a youth movement for young German aged from 10 to 14 years. It symbolises the common origin of all volunteers.

– the skeleton key: the insignia of the LSSAH which provided the cadre for the HJ Division. The 'Leibstandarte Adolf Hitler' was commanded until 1943 by 'Sepp' Dietrich whose surname translates as 'skeleton key' in colloquial German.

The 12th SS-Panzerdivision 'Hitlerjugend'

VEHICLES AND HEAVY WEAPONS ALLOTED TO THE DIVISION ON 1 JUNE 1944

ACTUAL ALLOTMENT	PROPORTION OF FULL COMPLEMENT
Tracked Armoured Vehicles	
– 50 Panther medium tanks ('As' and 'Gs')	61.5%
+ 22 tanks delivered from 1 to 6 June 1944	
– 98 PzKpfw IV medium tanks (mostly 'Hs')	96.9%
– two artillery observation tanks Art.Pz.Beob.Wg.III	50%
– 10 Jagdpanzer IV F AFVs	22%
– 12 Flak 38 20mm guns mounted on Czech Flakpanzer 38 (t) chassis	100%
– three Flakvierling 38 quadruple 20mm guns mounted on PzKpfw IV chassis	unknown.
– 12 'Wespe' self-propelled lPzH 18/2 100mm guns mounted on PzKpfw IV chassis	100%
– six 'Hummel' self-propelled sPzH 18/1 150mm howitzers mounted on PzKpfw III/IV chassis	100%
Armoured Vehicles (wheeled and half-tracked, soft-skinned and partially armoured)Total: 333	**85.3 %**
– eight-wheeled SdKfz 231 armoured vehicles	
– light armoured half-tracks	
(SdKfz 250/1, 250/4, 250/7, 250/8, 250/9, 250/10, and 250/11).	
– medium armoured half-tracks	
(SdKfz 251/1, 251/2, 251/4, 251/7, 251/8, 251/9, 251/10, 251/15 and 251/16).	
Four-wheeled SdKfz 223 radio vehicles are not included.	
– eight-wheeled SdKfz 232, SdKfz 250/3 and SdKfz 251/3.	
The regulation SdKfz 222 and 223 armoured vehicles were never delivered.	
Half-tracked vehicles (soft-skinned and partially armoured)	
– two Kettenrad tracked motorcycles	1.5%
– 41 1-5 ton prime movers (SdKfz 6, 10 and 11)	20.3%
The above includes:	
– 16 (?) self-propelled Flak 38 20mm guns (SdKfz 10/4)	
– 65 8-18 ton prime movers (SdKfz 7 and 9)	57.7%
The above includes:	
– nine self-propelled Flak 36 37mm guns (SdKfz 7/2)	
– four self-propelled Flakvierling quadruple 20mm guns (SdKfz 7/1).	
None of the 50 Maultier half-tracks were delivered.	
Wheeled Vehicles	
– 820 motorcycles and side cars	118.8%
– 505 light and cross-country cars	55.7%
– 418 light and medium cars	421.5%
– 240 cross-country trucks	19.2%
– 1,594 trucks and light trucks (including 288 Italian vehicles)	164.2%
Towed Artillery Pieces	
– 18 lFH 18/40 100mm howitzers	110.2%
– 12 sFH 18 150mm howitzers	including self-propelled guns)
– four K. 18 100mm guns	
Anti-tank Pieces	
– 31 towed 75mm Pak anti-tank guns	129%
Towed Anti-Aircraft Pieces	
– 12 Flak 36 88mm guns	100%
– 22 (?) Flak 38 20mm guns	unknown
Infantry Support Guns	
– 12 towed 150mm s/G. 33 heavy infantry guns	100%
– 20 towed 75mm lIG. 18 light infantry guns	74%
– four towed 76.2mm lKH. 290 (r) guns (captured from the Russians)	

ESTABLISHMENT ON 1 JUNE 1944

20,156 men. Including:
– 520 officers (shortfall: 144).
– 2,383 NCOs (shortfall: 2,192).
– 17,637 other ranks (overstaffing: 2,360), plus 1,103 auxiliaries (Russian 'Hiwis', Italians etc.)

THE 12TH SS-PANZERDIVISION 'HITLERJUGEND' ON 1 JUNE 1944

UNIT	NOTES	UNIT CO	ESTABLISHMENT (1)	PIPING COLOURS
Divisions-Kommando	Divisional	HQ SS-Brf. Witt (EL) / Division Commander		White
Divisions-Kartenstelle (mot)	Motorised Field Survey Platoon			White
SS-Divisions-Begleitkompanie (mot)	Motorised HQ Protection Company	SS-Ostuf. Gentrum	553	White
SS-Feldgendarmerie-Kompanie (mot) 12	Motorised Military Police Company	SS-Ostuf Buschausen		Orange
SS-Panzer-Regiment 12	Tank Regiment – armoured air defence section (12 x 20) – 1 battalion with command company – 4 'Panther' tank companies – motorised supply company – 1 battalion with command company, – 1 armoured air defence platoon (3 x quadruple 20mm guns), – 5 PzKpfw IV tank companies, maintenance and service company.	SS-Ostubat. Wünsche (RK)	2,301	Pink
SS-Panzerjäger-Abteilung (Sf) 12	Anti-Tank Battalion AFV Battalion – 3 Jagdpanzer IV companies or 75 towed anti-tank guns (understrength).	SS-Stubaf. Hanreich	516	Pink
SS-Panzergrenadier-Regiment 25	Armoured Infantry Regiment Motorised Infantry Regiment – Command company – 3 battalions of 3 panzergrenadier companies each. – 1 support company – 1 heavy infantry gun company (6 x 150mm) – 1 motorcycle recce company – 1 light air defence company (12 x 20mm) – 1 light engineer company	SS-Staf. K. Meyer (EL)	3,316	White
SS-Panzergrenadier-Regiment 26	Armoured Infantry Regiment – armoured recce company (operating SPWs) – 2 battalions (as Regiment 25) – 1 armoured battalion (SPW) of 3 panzergrenadier companies – 1 support company – 1 heavy infantry gun company (6 x 150mm) – 1 recce company – 1 light air defence company (12 x 20mm) – 1 light engineer company	SS-Ostubat. Monhke	3316	White
SS-Panzer-Aufklärungs-Abteilung 12	Armoured Recce Section – 1 armoured car company – 3 light SPW companies – 1 support company (medium SPWs) – 1 supply company	SS-Stubat. Bremer (RK)	938	Golden yellow
SS-Panzer Artillerie Regiment 12	Armoured Artillery Regiment – command battery – 1 light air defence section (4 x quadruple 20mm) – 1 command battery group including: – 2 self-propelled 6 x 100mm batteries, – 1 self-propelled 6 x 150mm battery – 1 command battery group, including: – 3 towed 6 x 100mm batteries – 1 4 x 100mm battery	SS-Ostubaf. Schröder	2,499	Scarlet
SS-Werfer-Abteilung (mot) 12	Motorised Rocket Launcher Unit Command battery, six launcher batteries and support unit.	SS-Hstuf. Müller	c 675	Scarlet
SS-Flak-Abteilung (mot) 12	Motorised Air Defence Section – command battery – 3 towed 4 x 88mm, 3 x 20mm batteries – 1 self-propelled 9 x 37mm battery – 1 searchlight unit (4 x 60mm) – 1 light motorised unit	SS-Stubat. Fend	c 940	Scarlet
SS-Panzer-Pionier-Bataillon 12	Armoured Engineer Battalion – armoured recce section – 1 armoured company (medium SPWs) – 2 light motorised companies – 2 bridging teams (B and K equipment)	SS-Stubat. S. Müller	c1,050	Black
SS-Panzer-Nachrichten-Abteilung 12	Armoured Signals Section – armoured signals company (wire) – armoured radio company (radio) – light armoured support unit	SS-Stubat. Pandel	519	Lemon yellow
SS-Panzerdivisions-Nachschubtruppen (mot) 12	Motorised Transport Group – 7 motorised transport companies. – 1 motorised supply company	SS-Stubat. Kolitz	976	Light blue
SS-Panzer-Instandsetzungs-Abteilung 12	Repair Section – 4 motorised field repair companies – 1 field depot echelon	SS-Stubat. Manthel	543	Light blue
SS-Wirtschafts-Bataillon (mot) 12	Motorised Supply Section – 1 motorised bakery company – 1 motorised butcher company – motorised quartermaster detachment	SS-Stubat. Dr. Kros	311	Light blue
SS-Sanitäts-Abteilung 12	Divisional Medical Section – 2 motorised medical companies – 3 ambulance sections – 1 health care unit	SS-Stubat. Dr. Schultz	660	Cornflower blue

1. Theoretical strength on 27 June 1944.

RK: *Ritterkreuz:* - Holder of the Knight's Cross.
EL: *Eichenlaub:* Holder of the Kight's Cross with oakleaves.
SPW: *Schützenpanzerwagen* (half-tracked armoured vehicle).

ACKNOWLEDGEMENTS

The authors wishe to thank all the specialists, militaria dealers and collectors who kindly supplied photographs and items from their collections to illustrate this book.

PHOTO CREDITS

US Airborne in Normandy: Christophe DESCHODT, Bertrand DESCHODT, Pierre SCHUBERT, François VAUVILLIER

British Red Berets in Normandy : Philippe CHARBONNIER, André PRINCE, Marcus COTTON

US Navy Beach Battalions in Normandy: Jon GAWNE

The D-Day GI: Philippe CHARBONNIER

12th SS Panzer Division in Normandy: Christophe DESCHODT, Jean-Marie MONGIN, Patrick LESIEUR. © PLST

Design: Philippe CHARBONNIER, Jean-Marie MONGIN, François VAUVILLIER
UK Co-ordinator: Alexandra GARDINER

ISBN : 2 908 182 32 7
Publisher's number : 2-908182.
Published by **Histoire & Collections**
19, avenue de la République.
75011 Paris, France.
Tél. : International (1) 40.21.18.20
Fax : International (1) 40.21.97.55

Editorial composition : *Macintosh II FX,*
Quadra 650, X Press and Adobe *Illustrator*
Photography : *SCIPE,* Paris.
Colour separation : *Point 11, Ogerault,* Paris.

Printed by *PPO,* Pantin, France,
on 30 April 1994

ISBN: *2 908 182 32 7*

HISTOIRE ET COLLECTIONS, P.O. Box 327, Poole, Dorset BH 15 2RG UK